H.J.M. Walenkamp, cover design
for the book 'Dreams'. by Olive
Schreiner, ± 1895

Cees Nooteboom

UNBUILT NETHERLANDS

Visionary projects by Berlage, Oud, Duiker, Van den Broek, Van Eyck, Hertzberger and others

H.J.M. Walenkamp, competition design for the cover of 'De Architect', 1895.

Cover
W.C. Bauer, competition design for a theatre seating 800, with motto 'Fiat', 1891.

First published in 1985 in the
United States of America by
RIZZOLI INTERNATIONAL
PUBLICATIONS, INC.
597 Fifth Avenue, New York, New
York 10017

LC numer: 84-43105
ISBN: 0-8478-0593-X

Library of Congress Cataloging in
Publication Data

Nooteboom, Cees, 1933-
Unbuilt Netherlands.

Translation of: Nooit gebouwd
Nederland.
Bibliography: p.
1. Architectural drawing--19th
century--Netherlands.
2. Architectural drawing--20th
century--Netherlands.
I. Title.
NA2706.N4N613 1985
720'.22'2 84-43105
ISBN 0-8478-0593-X

Composition
Cees de Jong
Frank den Oudsten
Dick van Woerkom

Advice
Nederlands Documentatiecentrum
voor de Bouwkunst,
Amsterdam

Essay
Cees Nooteboom

Captions
Frank den Oudsten
Wim de Wit
Dick van Woerkom

Photography
Frank den Oudsten

Translation
From Dutch into English
Mrs Adrienne Dixon, Colchester,
England

Design
Cees de Jong,
vorm + kleur grafisch ontwerpers,
Amsterdam

Typesetting:
I.G.S., Eindhoven

Lithography:
Ginsa S.A., Barcelona, Spain

Printed by:
A.G. Grijelmo S.A., Bilbao Spain

First published in The Netherlands
in 1980.
Title: Nooit Gebouwd Nederland.
Re-published in 1983.

J.J.B. Franswa, study for a theatre,
± 1924.

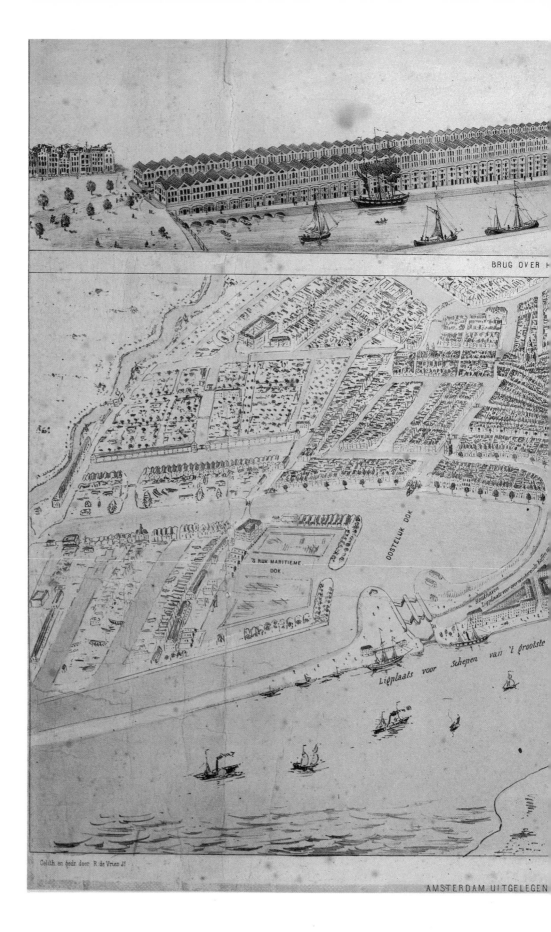

J. Galman, Bridge over the IJ, 1857.

BRUG OVER H

OOSTELIJK DOK

'S RIJK MARITIEME. DOK.

Ligplaats voor Schepen van 't grootste

Gelith en gedr door R de Vries Jr

AMSTERDAM UITGELEGEN

N J. GALMAN

WESTELIJK DOK.

groote   zee - Stoomboten

Noord Hollandsch kanaal

ONTWERP VAN J. GALMAN.

Uitgegeven door Frans Buffa en Zonen te Amsterdam. 1857.

Unbuilt Netherlands is a visual book about architecture. On the basis of never executed designs, it gives an outline of the development of Dutch architecture in the period 1850 - 1985.

The book contains designs that never got further than the drawingboard because they were too fantastical, too advanced, or impracticable for technical, financial or political reasons. Contrary to expectation, true utopian designs, not intended to be realized, appeared to be virtually non-existent in the Netherlands. Unbuilt Netherlands demonstrates that the Netherlands might have looked very different, and presents the designs in chronological order. The time period can be subdivided into four parts, each defined by dates that are important both from a political and an architectural historical point of view: 1918, 1945, and 1968.

In making our selection we have not attempted to be comprehensive. The book is not an inventory of everything that was designed and not built. It is a selection, a subjective choice, from those designs which we regard, for reasons of history and quality, as highlights in the history of Dutch architecture.

Unbuilt Netherlands is a depository of architectural design in the Netherlands over the last 135 years and wishes at the same time to be a plea for the quality of our built environment, for greater (political) courage in decision taking on the part of patrons, and for a climate of design in which the imagination rules, in which there is room for the architect's secret: space.

The editors.

Hannah Arendt

The world is the dwelling place for people during their stay on earth.

P.J.H. Cuypers, design for St Willibrord's Church-without-the Veste, Amsteldijk, Amsterdam, 1864-1899.

In the Church of St Willibrord, Cuypers wanted to realize a medieval ideal, that of a church with as many towers as possible: two on either side of the façade, two on either side of both transept façades, and one over the crossing (the place where nave and transepts cross).
Just as in the Middle Ages this ideal was usually unattainable owing to lack of money, Cuypers ideal also got no further than the drawing board. The church was built, but with only one tower, the one over the crossing.

The essence of a never-built building is that it isn't there. It is invisible because it doesn't exist. No one can live in it, no one can walk past it, on one can clean it, on one will be able to remember it, because it has never existed. An unborn child will never change the world, an unwritten book will never make us think, the unpainted picture will never be photographed. And yet there is a difference between the never-written and the never-built. The unwritten is at most visible in

8

ONTWERP TOT UITBREIDING VAN AMSTERDAM LANGS HET NOORDZEE·KANAAL DOOR A. HUET INGᵉ

GEZIGT VAN UIT SCHELLINGWOUDE OP DE BRUG OVER HET NIEUWE Y-DOK

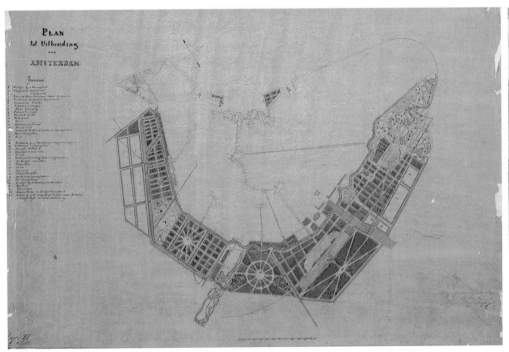

A. Huet, development plan for Amsterdam, along the North Sea Canal, 1874.

Huet realized that as a result of the digging of the North Sea Canal, (opened in 1876) the harbour would slowly be moved from the eastern part of the city to the west. For this reason, he designed a development plan for Amsterdam alongside the new canal. In his view, the IJ no longer needed to serve as harbour and could become a closed dock.

Elevated railway from Commelinstraat to Zwanenburgwal via Waterlooplein, 1883. At the end of the 19th century, Amsterdam, like all large cities in Europe, wants a city railway. However, it is obvious that because of the nature of the soil, an undergrond railway system is impossible in Amsterdam.

note form, one can have some idea of what the writer would have done *if* he had done what he intended to do; no more. In architecture it is different; there we know for sure what the architect would have built if he had built what he wanted: stone or concrete, steel or aluminium, the height of the roof, the width of the façade, the form and the colour; the entire structure is there, it has been conceived, designed, drawn, only it has not become matter, it is there and it is not there. And this completes the contradiction in my opening sentence: the building is not there because it does not exist and is therefore not visible as a building, yet at the same time it is there in a way because it is visible as a design, as a drawing.

What this book shows is what the Netherlands *could* have looked like, but also, and this is the breath-taking paradox, what it *did* look like. The unbuilt forms part of a culture just as much as the built, it exists as thought, as response, as idea, as wish. Even to Freud the wish was father to the thought, we express ourselves through our wishes, and wishes, desires, ideas and dreams are seldom expressed more clearly, more meticulously than in not-built architecture. This is not true of all the ideas and designs in this book, but more than any other discipline, architecture demands precision, measurements, figures. If it is built, the building will stand somewhere, it will occupy a certain surface area on the ground and also a certain volume of space. The spatial emptiness will, thus and thus, from the ground to

J.C. Van Niftrik, development plan for Amsterdam, 1866.

The population growth since ± 1850 made it necessary for Amsterdam to have a municipal development plan; this was the only way to prevent uncontrolled building outside the Singelgracht. Civil engineer Van Niftrik designs a grand plan: all around the old city he lays a belt which he divides into neighbourhoods for the various classes, separated from one another by parks. This division — working class districts in the east and west and middle class districts in the south — fits in with the geography of the classes in the old city and can still be seen in outline in today's development. The plan was doomed to fail from the start, because in several places it extends far beyond the municipal boundaries.

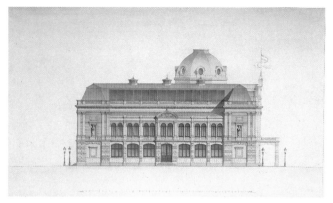

L.H. Eberson, design for a new museum in Amsterdam, 1875.

On the occasion of the 50th anniversary of the Kingdom of the Netherlands in 1863, a committee was set up to prepare the foundation of the King Willem II Museum, wich was to house the state collection (which was at that time kept under rather poor conditions in the Trippenhuis), the collection of the City of Amsterdam and the Van der Hoop collection.
It was envisaged that the museum would be a monument to our national glory in the 17th century, thereby enhancing the self-awareness of the young independent state. The committee organized a competition, for which nineteen entries were received. The award winners were: Architects Lange from Munich and P.J.H. Cuypers (first and second prizes). The competition did not result in a contract, however, because a furious quarrel developed as to the style in which such a national museum should be built. The general consensus was that it should be a truly 'Dutch' style, which meant, for instance, that there must be no Greek

colonnades; whether this referred to neo-Gothic or Renaissance style was a question on which no agreement could be reached. In order to break the deadlock, the architects Godefroy and Eberson were asked to submit plans. Godefroy refused and the design sent in by Eberson in 1864 was considered unsuitable.

this or that height, be filled, people will no longer be able to walk through it, they will run up against matter, something will be visible. The strange thing about the unbuilt is that it says something about us in two ways. Firstly it shows what someone would have liked to build – the wish; secondly, it expresses equally sharply and precisely, what was not built; the refusal, the no. There are many reasons for building something and there are probably even more reasons for saying no. If one is to call that which is built, all that has been constructed by man since the beginning of time, the canonical history of architecture, one could say that what we are dealing with in this book is an apocryphal history. It is not the authentic history, because if it were, these buildings would have been built, and yet it is an essential part of history because it states and demonstrates, perhaps even better than the history of what was actually built, what architects were occupied with.

But what are architects exactly? The answer is as long as all built buildings placed side by side. They are philosophers, inspired utopians, practical men of action, dreamers in steel and concrete, lunatics, crafty manipulators of the will of speculators, people with delusions of grandeur, servants of the people, cultural barbarians, prophets, geniuses, copy-cats, thieves, artists. The history of architecture is at the same time the history of bad architecture, for there is one thing which all architects, good or bad, have in common: what they build, if they build it, can literally not be avoided; it is there.

Anyone who does not want to see Rembrandt's Nightwatch, can avoid doing so by *not* going into the Rijksmuseum, but anyone wanting to cycle from the Spiegelgracht to the Concertgebouw, must pass through Cuypers' archway under the Rijksmuseum, whether he likes it or not. And although the architect, like the painter and the poet, is a product of history and of society, the relative inescapability of what he produces still makes him, for better or for worse, an obtrusive fellow citizen. We cannot avoid meeting

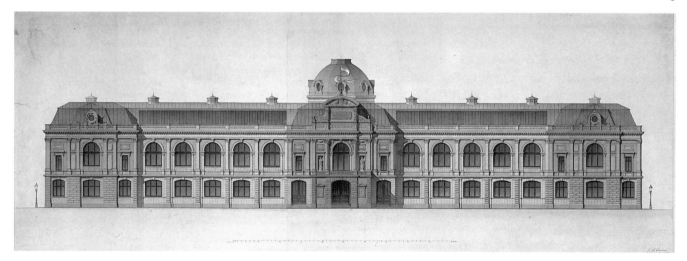

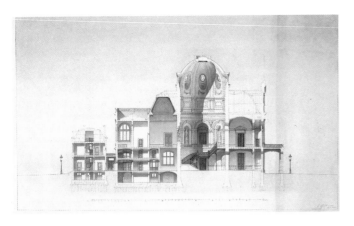

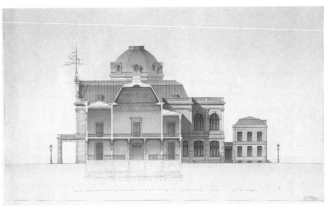

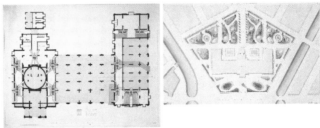

In 1875 a new attempt was made to find a suitable design for a national museum. The Minister for Home Affairs invited three architects, Cuypers, Vogel and Eberson, to submit designs. Cuypers won and was given the contract. Eberson's design was considered to be the worst of the three, because it was conceived not in Dutch style but in Louis Seize, and was moreover too reminiscent of several recently completed buildings (cf: F.J. Duparc, One Century of Fighting for Dutch Cultural Heritage, The Hague, 1975, page 101).

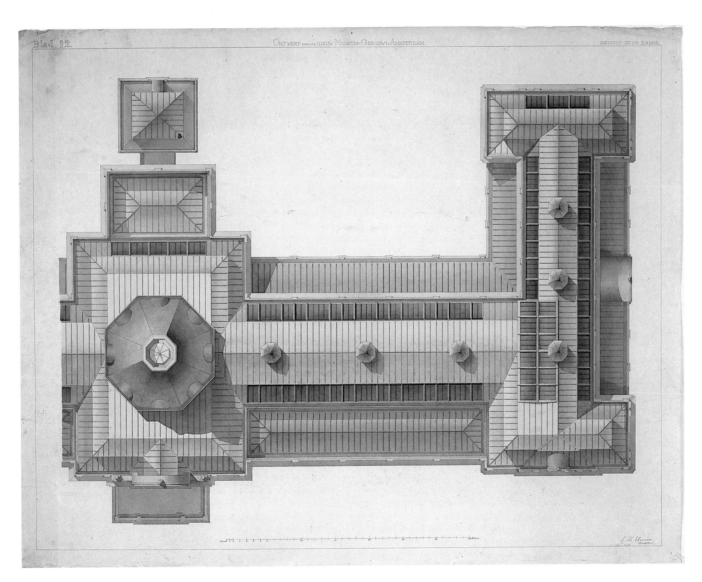

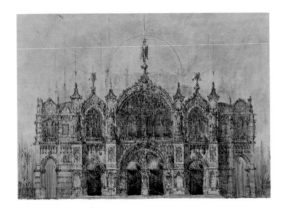

W.C. Bauer, competition entry for
a concert hall, motto: 'Preludium',
1889.

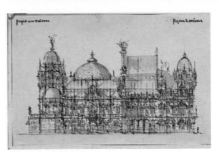

W.C. Bauer, competition entry for
a theatre of 800 seats, motto:
'Fiat', 1891.

his work. It is always and everywhere around us. Even when we
don't look at it we still see it.

Anyone entering a library, a hospital, a church, a post office, a
station, a deprtment store, a theatre, enters an imagined, designed,
and eventually built space. Anyone walking around a city at his own
pace is subjected to perspectives, to articulations of space, vistas,
steep walls towering above him, to reflections, divisions, emptinesses
and fullnesses which not he but someone else has invented and built.
He sees, often without realising it, references to a past of which
even the builder was no longer aware. He sees the architecture of
need and poverty, of hope and defeat, he sees architecture lost in its
own history and architecture reflecting the slimy underside of his
own or a bygone age.

And beyond all this he sees – or perhaps he doesn't see, but that
doesn't matter because what has been built is there anyway – the
architect who has become submerged in his building (the builder
becomes the building he builds), a master, a servant, a free man or
someone whose hands were tied by regents, entrepreneurs, or
simply by lack of talent.

There are cities that have built themselves, cities whose form and
situation have been prescribed by nature; some cities have acquired
their face because of the coercive will of a ruler, others because of
the fear of an enemy. Ever since Vitruvius, people have written
about architecture and this accumulated literature could keep a
respectable reader occupied for a lifetime. He would discover that a
number of problems may have changed in form or intensity, but not
in essence. Even before the advent of the car there were huge
traffic problems, even in the past citizens needed roofs over their
heads, even in antiquity there had to be public buildings in which to
carry out public functions, and within a given built-up area people
have always felt the desire to get from A to B, preferably by the
most direct route.

The archetype of town planning is expounded in the lucid language of
the Enlightenment by the Jesuit Laugier (*Observations sur l'Architecture*,

W.C. Bauer, competition entry for
the façade of a church, 1892.

PROJET D'UN THÉÂTRE.

' "Fiat" is a beautiful design. Looking at it closely, one feels one is entering a whole new domain, an immense field confined only by the natural laws of harmony and composition, in which one does not have to stumble over the boundary posts of various stylistic periods, nor over the barbed wire entanglements of units and modules. (...)

"Fiat" has jumped across the obstacles, after first having filled its pockets with traditional motifs, which it then proceeded to sift conscientiously. After the sifting, little was left: a bit of Moorish, a bit of Gothic, and some.

With these three elements, and much else of its own invention, an ensemble was created that can be called magnificent, full of beautiful compositions, harmonious groupings, witty detail, all of it governed by a strong sense of the whole.'

W. Kr(omhout), De Opmerker, 1892, page 12.

W.C. Bauer, competition entry for a workers' congress building, motto 'La Révolte', 1893.

Bauer is particularly fascinated by Byzantine and Islamic architecture, which he knows well from the descriptions and sketches of his brother M. Bauer. He tries to combine oriental features in his own architectural designs. This was possible because in his first few years as an architect, Bauer did not receive a single commission and devoted himself exclusively to sending in competition designs. Most juries did not appreciate this arbitrary apllication of un-Dutch stylistic

features. In the jury report of a competition for a workers' congress building, the following remark is made about Bauer's design 'La Révolte': 'It reminds one more of a building of pre-Christian, oriental origin than of a building that meets the demands of the closing years of the nineteenth century.' (Architectura 2, 1894, page 192).

The Hague 1765) when he says: 'Anyone who can design a park will have no difficulty in drawing the plan according to which a city must be built, in conformity with its size and situation. Squares, intersections and streets are required. Regularity and capriciousness are both needed, agreement and contrast, coincidences which create variety in the overall picture; a great orderliness in the details, confusion, force and tumult in the whole'.

From Laugier there are lines to be drawn, not so much in an ideological sense as in the sense of involvement. Lines leading to l'Enfant, who designed the great plan of Washington, to Le Corbusier, Taut, Hilbersheimer, Wijdeveld, van Eesteren. However much they may differ among themselves, in many respects they have one obvious point in common: their involvement. No longer the architecture of one building, brilliant or otherwise, but the architect who is concerned with the lot of a whole community. The architect becomes the philosopher of society, and is at the same time – if his vision is to become reality – given an opportunity to determine

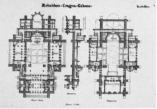

how, and sometimes also where, thousands of people will live. The power of someone who, whether or not with the backing of a monarch or under the umbrella of a government, is allowed to change a city or even to build one from scratch, is both fascinating and frightening. Society is at the mercy of such a person. Politicians, having been elected, can subsequently be thrown overboard, but we must continue to walk, look, live, eat, make love, sleep in the streets, city centres, parks, houses and garrisons which the architects have designed. The stage scenery is there, and we cannot change it. If it is true that all the world's a stage, the action must take place here, against this backdrop and these wings, in this space, determined not by ourselves but by someone else.

Antonio de Pietro Averlino worked as a sculptor on the doors of the baptistry in Florence and designed the great hospital in Milan, as well as Bergamo Cathedral. Before 1465 he had already written a

H.P. Berlage, design for an artist's studio house, 1888.

textbook in twenty-five volumes, in which he created, for the powerful Sforza family, the ideal city of Sforzinda.
Utopian science fiction, perhaps, but after Averlino there were many more such people, men who were given an opportunity to convert their ideas about society into designs that subsequently became fixed in stone or steel, or, by contrast, into the demolition hammer that brought down whatever stood in the way of the new ideas.

'Aen d'Aemstel en aen t' Y,
daer doet sich heerlyck open
sy die, als Keiserin, de kroon
draeght van Europe,'

('On the banks of Amstel and IJ'
There opens out most gloriously
she who as Empress wears
the crown of Europe.')
wrote Vondel, but the city rulers of the nineteenth century thought they knew better and closed what was open. They made the city blind in both eyes, no longer able to see what it had been and from what it had arisen: a city on the water, a water city. In one blow, the natural symbiosis was broken; with the blind wall of Central

H.P. Berlage, design for a vestibule to a royal residence, ± 1885.

Station, blind men sealed off the city from its most essential element: water. She could no longer, like Lisbon on the Tagus or Rio de Janeiro on the ocean, lie like a coquettish old lady on her sofa and watch out over the past whence had come her character and her riches, no, she was locked up within her narrow fortress until finally she had to climb across the last remaining cinctures and saw her splendid concentricity destroyed.

Apartment blocks proliferated like a disease all over the polders that had once been the heart of Amstel-land, and condemned the inhabitants to an environment from which they had to try as best they could to find the way back to the natural heart of their city, across obstacles and barriers which more recent, though equally blind, rulers had put up.

There are two reasons why Amsterdam began to think about a new Exchange building in the 1880's. Firstly, the Exchange built on the Dam by Zocher in 1843 was in poor condition. But the main reason was the desire to fill in the Dam canal in order to create a boulevard, running from Central Station (the construction of which had started in 1882) to the Dam Square, and Zocher's Exchange stood in the way of such a boulevard.

The Dam was eventually partly filled in, but the boulevard was never made. In 1884 a competition was organized inviting designs for an Exchange on the filled-in site.

The winner, L.M. Cordonnier from Lille, was heavily criticized for alleged plagiarism: his design looks exactly like the town hall of La Rochelle. This caused so much argument that in 1888 the City Council decided not to proceed with an Exchange at all. In 1897 Alderman Treub decided that an Exchange would have to be built after all, and invited his friend H.P. Berlage to design one.

What might have been done instead, can be seen, albeit only in a dream, on pages four and five, the design of a bridge over the IJ by J. Galman in 1857. He is a favourite of mine, this contemporary of Tollens, Huet and Multatuli. There were probably laws standing in the way, and practical objections, but I cannot keep my eyes off that drawing. Like the arrow of a Zen archer, his bridge goes straight into the bull's eye, flying with the poise of a champion shot' into the heart of Amsterdam. Can you see yourself walking there on a fine spring morning? The water trembles and quivers on both sides. You look out over the 'Moorings for ships of the greatest tonnage and large ocean liners', at the highest point of the bridge you can see the green of distant polders and the turning sails of windmills; straight ahead are Old Church, West Church and South Church, and then you literally enter the city, as you are led, in a long, logical line, down the empty Damrak, bordered by elms or lime trees, to the navel of this cosmos, the Dam. But the bridge has never existed, and therefore, someone who might have been you or me − someone who walked over that bridge on a spring morning − has never existed either.

We were not yet born and yet we were already robbed of something. Not only of a connecting link − whether it was 'possible' to build it doesn't matter any longer − but also of a view, and a sensation. On 3 May 1953 you might have fallen in love on that bridge with someone who, just like you, stood looking out over the hazy water. Before we ourselves are allowed to decide over our lives, much has already been decided for us. The above may be regarded as nonsense, but whether it is or is not cannot be proved. The designer has power, if his building is built. The person who, for whatever reason, rejects the design, thereby destroying it as a potential building, also has power. The planner, as interior decorator of the cosmos, the builder as the manager of human destiny, as the herald of yet another new age, the planner as the exponent of a political or economic system, the planner as rubble remover or demolition man; these we meet in history again and again.

They are called Gropius or Haussmann, Maimont or Saarinen, Berlage or Van Ravesteyn, and they have one thing in common: they busy themselves with that which, once it is there, will be an inescapable part of the environment in which we have to spend our lives. Not only do they 'arrange' the external environment, the urban cosmos in which we move, but they also concern themselves with the 'internal' environment in which we live, the closed universe of the private dwelling. He who designs a thousand identical windows

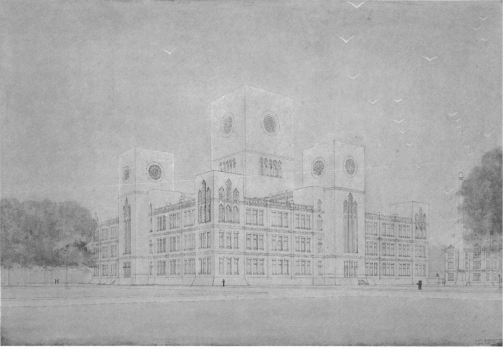

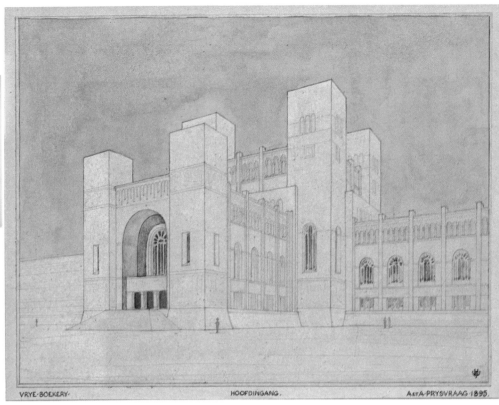

H.J.M. Walenkamp, competition design for a public library, motto 'The Free Bookery', 1895.

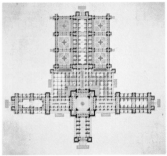

Walenkamp's design for a library was entered for the competition sponsored by the 'Architectura et Amicitia' Society, in which De Bazel also took part (see pages 21, 22 and 23). However, Walenkamp did not complete his design in time.
Five years later, the fully worked-out design was published in the architectural journal 'Bouwkundig Weekblad' (B.W. 1900/page 300).

VRYE·BOEKERY·   HOOFDINGANG.   A.et A·PRYSVRAAG·1895.

for a thousand identical homes, does not design a thousand times the same view, but a thousand times exactly the same size of view. He who builds a thousand identical bedrooms cannot prevent the inhabitants of Apartment No. 391 from making love on the kitchen floor, but he has nevertheless somehow influenced the sex life of a thousand families he does not know.

A mass society probably requires mass solutions, but I would shudder at the thought of having such power, at so many possibilities accompanied by so many restraints. I think one needs to have courage and be very firmly convinced of one's own ideas in order to intervene so drastically in the lives of one's fellow beings. Every design, even the one that is not executed, is such an intervention. To the architect who, after long deliberation and calculation, finally commits his ideas to paper, and subsequently submits and presents his explicit self-confidence, the building is of course a real building. And real buildings, as he knows from history, cannot easily be got rid of, any more than can ideas about the city-as-a-whole. In architecture we inherit the past, both the good and the bad — and errors have a long life.

The architect Hippodamus, a faithful follower of Pythagoras, who designed the agora at Miletus and built closed private dwellings which had no logical connection with the rest of the town and in which simple possibilities for communication between the residential and the public areas of the town were lacking, had great influence on the eventual planning of the Forum Romanum, which in its turn became the model for numerous colonial settlements in the endlessly

expanding Roman empire. Le Corbusier declares in Modulor 2 that he gets his inspiration from Hindu and pre-Socratic sources, and according to Sibyl Moholy-Nagy (*Matrix of Man*, Praeger, New York 1968), Mies van der Rohe's interest in the 24-foot module and Buckminster Fuller's predilection for the magic triangle are connected, via the secret routes of earliest history, with Sumerian-Babylonian numerology in which there are echoes from pre-historic matriarchy and in which six was the perfect number. J.E. Cirlot, in his *Diccionario de los Simbolos Tradicionales* (English edition Routlegde & Kegan Paul, 5th impression 1976) is as voluble: 'The symbolism of architecture is founded upon 'correspondences' between various patterns of spatial organization, consequent upon the relationships, on the abstract plane, between architectural structures and the organized pattern of space. While the basic pattern of architectural relationships provides the primary symbolism, secondary symbolic meanings are derived from the appropriate selection of individual forms, colours and materials, and by the relative importance given to the various elements forming the architectural whole (function, height, etc.)'

'Look at what isn't there,' you might say with the poet Nijhoff, except that in this case it isn't about words but about buildings. In everything we see, and in this book that means the unbuilt (which *really* isn't there), distant legacies of magical and mystical theories, lost to conscious thought, play a part and are expressed in forms, colours and proportions.

If Cuypers' cathedral had been built (page 8) and we could have walked past it, how many of us would then have known what

K.P.C. de Bazel, competition
design for a public library, motto
'1114', 1895.

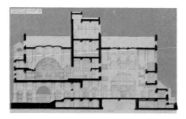

The Jubilee competition, set up by
the 'Architectura et Amicitia'
Society in 1895 on the occasion of
its fortieth anniversary, did not, in
the opinion of jury members
Cuypers, Peters and Berlage,
produce the grand result that
might have been expected of such
a competition. De Bazel's design
was not considered good enough
either. The jury called it clever, but
rejected it because of what it
regarded as an incorrect surface
plan. Moreover, they speak of a
'dubious monumentality', owing to,
among other things, 'strange, here
and there intended ornamentation,
reminiscent of woodcarving'
(Architectura, 1896, p. 181) and
to its large wall areas with small
windows.

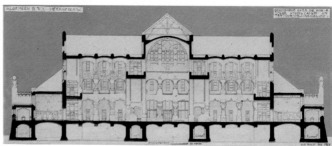

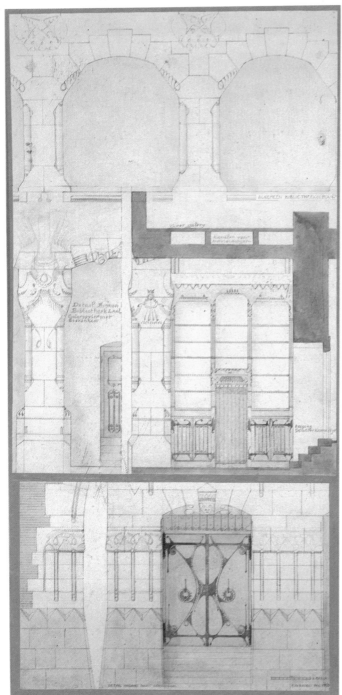

Cuypers, like his model Viollet-le-Duc, knew very well: that the
symbol of the magic triangle, inherited from earlier religions and here
visible in the pointed arches, the three doors in the facade and the
ogive, which is nothing but a triangle with curved sides, represents
the Holy Trinity? The large central tower over the crossing of nave
and transepts stands for the mountain of Jupiter, the two frontal
towers are the two peaks of the mountain of Mars, related to the
symbols of Gemini, Janus and the number 2. The three doors in the
West front are faith, hope and charity, the large rose window is the
Lake of Life in which heaven and earth meet.

Should this cathedral therefore have been built? I am not saying it
should, but I would have been very pleased if, on a drizzly autumn
day, I could have strolled through this late Gothic echo into my
medieval past. For this is also a function of buildings: they preserve
the memory of the past, or, to say it more paradoxically, they even
preserve the memory of the forgotten. In that sense it is of course
no coincidence that there is no cathedral on the bank of the Amstel.
Building a Gothic cathedral in Amsterdam in the nineteenth century
would have been an act of memory, and the Dutch don't build for
memory.

At least De Bazel's design was much appreciated by his contemporaries, perhaps too much so, as is shown by an appeal in the journal 'Architectura' (4, 1896, p. 195), requesting the person who had stolen the design from an award-winners' exhibition to return it.

Berlage's disapproval does not, in the end, prevent him from using De Bazel's ideas in his design for the Amsterdam Exhange;

IO METER

K. de BAZEL   DEC. 1895

*(1897/1898) in which the same
flat wall surface and the specific
ornamentation can be seen again.
(see: A.W. Reinink, K.P.D. de
Bazel, Architect, Leiden, 1965).*

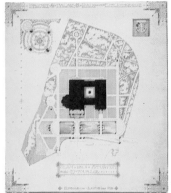

W. Kromhout, competition design
for the Peace Palace, The Hague,
1906.

At the Peace Conference at The
Hague in 1899, a permanent
Court of Arbitration was set up,
which was to mediate in
international conflicts so as to
maintain world peace. This
permanent court had to be
provided with a residence in The
Hague: the Palace of Peace. The
New York businessman Carnegie
having donated one and a half
million dollars, an international
competition was organized. Two
hundred and sixteen entries were
received. In a record time of ten

days, the jury examined all the
designs and reached a final verdict.
The winner was the Frenchman,
L.M. Cordonnier, an old
acquaintance of the Dutch because
twenty years previously he had
won the competition for the
Amsterdam Exchange. Once again
a storm of protest arose, this time
not because of plagiarism (see
page 18) but because his design
was thought to have far exceeded
the stipulated construction budget.
Even so, he received the
commission.

Astrological calculations, mystical allusions, vanished though still
present kabbalistic and numerological preoccupations, magical
memories, rational legacies. To anyone who wants to (can) see it, it
is all still present in architecture, a veiled collective burden which we
drag with us on our journey through time.

'O che dolce cosa e questa prospettiva!' exclaimed an enraptured
Paolo Ucello, thereby expressing the ecstasy of Renaissance man
who had discovered himself as the centre of everything. We, who
are beginning to suspect, on the basis of other Renaissance
discoveries that we wander instead like nameless stowaways through
the endless halls of the universe, can perhaps feel only some nostalgia
at such exclamations, but it must have been so wonderful: to be
swept into the big, dramatic world-square and to meet yourself
there as the measure of all things – and therefore as unique. For
the organization of the city it had, at any rate,
revolutionary/consequences. 'One of the functions of architecture',
says Edmund N. Bacon (*Design of Cities*, Thames & Hudson, 1974),
'is the creation of spaces to intensify the drama of existence'.
Life as a drama, the city as a theatre, and the 'new' man of the
Renaissance as at once actor and spectator. The theatre, the
enclosed area for action, became a great work of perspective; on
the stage it achieved the Renaissance aim of building everything
around man, of demonstrating that all the proportions of the
universe are based on the measurements of the human body.'
'...There came a moment when painters, decorators and architects
designed the same area according to the same rules of spatial
organization and created a pattern of civilization which imposed itself
on the whole world and of which the charm has not yet been

H.P. Berlage, design for a
Beethoven House, Bloemendaal,
1908.

At the beginning of this century the
adoration of Beethoven had
reached such a peak that plans
were made to found a Beethoven
Society which would build a
concert hall in which only works by
Beethoven were to be performed.
The building of a separate concert
hall was considered necessary
because none of the existing halls
was thought suitable for a
successful rendering of Beethoven's
music: 'the harmony of the notes is
disturbed by the over-ornate
architectural environment'. The
brochure about the proposed
Beethoven House (written by W.
Hutschenruyter, Amsterdam,
1908) therefore eagerly quotes
Berlage's remarks that the
architecture of concert halls should
be pure of composition and
modestly decorated. 'For only then
will the visitors receive that lofty
impression that music can bestow,
because they will be in an
environment which — like temples
and churches in the past — does
not obtrude but which, for that
very reason, radiates a sense of
consecration in harmony with the
spirit of the music'. (page 28)

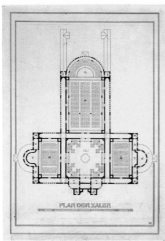

The site intended for the Beethoven
House (in the dunes of
Kennemerland) had been specially
chosen in order that the visitor, on
his way to the concert, could be
suitably inspired beforehand. The
dune landscape, which was to
remain visible from the concert
hall, would help to create the right
atmosphere.

exhausted, for what tourists come to look for in Florence, Siena or
Venice is not only architectural beauty but also a specific art of
living.' (*Perspectief*, Pierre Descargues, Landshoff 1976).

One of the tourists entering the stone stage of the 'theatre' of the
Piazza San Marco is W.C. Bauer. How he arrived there for the first
time I do not know, but I think that he, like me, must have come out
of the Calle Contarina or the San Moise, and was therefore, across
the empty expanse of the square, confronted head-on with San
Marco. What kind of shock this produced can be seen on pages 13,
14 and 15. The voluptuous shapes of the Byzantine domes, the
luxurious, oriental superabundance, have never been allowd to
become stone and mosaic under our grey skies, we shall never sit in
one of the eight hundred seats, never listen to Diepenbrock in his
concert hall. Paper it will remain, this exotic splendour. The juries
made it clear to him that he had 'fallen out of his century', but what
they probably meant was that such voluptuous exuberance does not
belong here.
'And all these buildings will be beautiful and noble,
And art will be rich, mightily rich.
That is the art of the future!
Architect! Prepare thyself!'
This is what Bauer wrote in *Architectura* in 1894, eight years before
he was found dead in his garden shed by Frederik van Eeden.
'Last Sunday I went to see poor W.B. and found him hanging in his
garden shed. Poor, fine, sensitive man with his great gifts. It was a
lugubrious stain on this joyous, hopeful, life-enhancing spring. Yet it
did not depress me.'

H.P. Berlage, development plan for The Hague, 1908.

In 1907 Berlage was asked to design a development plan for The Hague. Berlage took the structure of the existing city as his guideline. 'As the street plan of old The Hague consists largely of a system of streets crossing at right-angles, it seemed obvious to apply the same principle. However, it immediately became clear that the radial or diagonal street could not be dispensed with, owing to the demands of traffic. ... In any case, it seems to me that this feature generally enhances the town scene'. Berlage placed the Foundation for Internationalism in the North East, completely separate from the city. De Bazel

had already planned a World Capital for this Foundation in 1905, and Berlage literally took the plan over from him. In this World Capital, the Foundation for Internationalism hoped to establish a centre where international congresses in the fields of education, hygiene and economics could be held. In the opinion of the Foundation, a study of these three areas would greatly benefit world peace, and would be a useful complement to the Permanent Court of Arbitration which could operate only in judicial matters.

'Great gifts...' – he had those, certainly, but apart from a few villas for friends, his legacy consists chiefly of unexecuted designs. He could not and would not submit to what we now call market forces. He sought 'an art that will be as beautiful as the scent of heather after a sultry day, luxuriant as the rose, budding in the first days of summer, mighty as a summer forest and delicate as the butterfly that has cast off its caterpillar guise, tingling with life like the jubilant song of a free bird.'

What bombast, you might say, if you did not know he would pay for these high-flown ideals with his life. Gorter believed in workers 'who would dance in silver rows on the ocean shore', Bauer believed in 'the well-being of all, an aim that must be achieved. Then they will build palaces, in order to let those around them participate in the joy of life; the poor, who for so many centuries did not know life and who now, at last, can see its beauty...'

It is easy to sneer cynically at this in retrospect. We know that there is dancing on the ocean shore, but only in discotheques (in Torremolinos) and that the ideal of beauty is, to most people, represented on the television screen. We can shake our spoilt heads at all those world improvers of good family who, from their Gooiland villas, were so busily planning to raise the proletariat – after a brave struggle the outcome of which was assured – to the light of beauty. The material struggle has to some extent been won,

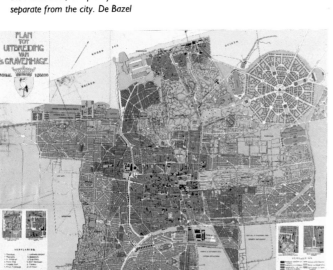

W. Kromhout, competition design for a new plan for the Dam Square, Amsterdam, motto 'Fancy', 1907.

After the demolition in 1903 of Zocher's old Exchange, the Dam was no longer a square. Part of the square wall had disappeared, leaving only a large gap. Something badly needed to be done to restore the appearance of the most important square in the Netherlands.
In 1906 the City Council of Amsterdam invited designs for a 'general plan and aesthetic design for the Dam and surrounding areas, to conform with the demands of traffic and appearance'. It was the intention that the central area of the square would also be built on. As usual, the competition ran into problems. The design by J.M. van der Mey, which was selected as the best, did not receive an award because the designer had not obeyed the instruction that all entries should be executed in Indian ink. Of the

design by Kromhout, the jury (which included Berlage, Ingenohl and Salm) remarked: 'Because of its grand conception, this architecture must be considered less suitable for the Dam Square, partly also with a view to its financial feasibility'. (Bouwkundig Weekblad 28, 1908, page 567). The solution for the central Dam area was reached only after the second world war, by the decision to put up a 'monument to the fallen'. Kromhout's drawing shown here is a later elaboration of his competition entry.

H.J.M. Walenkamp, design for a hotel on the Dam, Amsterdam, 1911-1912.

but almost a century later the Socialist Party, which was, after all, born from this *élan vital*, has still not succeeded in formulating a cultural policy in which it can believe and in which there burns even the smallest spark of the passion that glows from the testimonies of Bauer, Gorter, Henriette Roland Holst-Van der Schalk and others.

What is so striking in many of Bauer's, Walenkamp's, De Bazel's and Kromhout's designs is their loftiness and, in some cases, their intense passion for decoration. We are here, to speak with Jan Romein, 'at the shear between two cultures' and, as he puts it, 'From the sublime to the ridiculous it is always only one step, the same as from the profound to the senseless.' To demonstrate the truth of this he quotes a text by Jan Veth – a contemporary of the people of *Architectura*, in which Veth discusses a drawing by Toorop: '...quivering undulations; undulations of lines that... surge, swell, swirl and sing, like bubbling fountains, seeking a way until they rise in broad rhythms... swaying lines... lines that writhe and shrink, sob and struggle, twist and burst asunder, kneeling in prayer, plunging in flight... scream-lines of loud reverberation, pang-lines of sonorous flight...' It remains, again in retrospect, a strange combination, these socially conscious, loftily humanitarian aspirations and the neurotic-aesthetic way in which they are phrased; a torridness of expression, drawing, decoration and design that must have been far removed from the proletarian reality of those days, which was, after all, the object of concern. One can see it everywhere.

The 'pang-lines of sonorous flight' in Bauer's church façade of 1892, the ethereal symbolism of book jackets, prints and designs by Walenkamp, of titles such as Berlage's 'Pantheon of Mankind', De Bazel's and Lauweriks' rhetoric derived from the sexual sphere, the symbolism of Kromhout's truncated tower, the swelling cupolas in Bauer's designs — especially the inviting entrances and thrusting towers...'

This last quotation comes from a booklet entitled *Architectura, Nederlandse Architectuur 1893-1918*, published by the Architecture-Museum Foundation on the occasion of the exhibition of the same name. It is essential reading for anyone interested in this period and in the people who played major parts in it — Bauer, De Bazel, Lauweriks, Walenkamp, Kromhout, as is its companion booklet, *Americana* which deals with the period 1880-1930.

The writers of *Architectura* point out correctly that the above — mentioned architects have no place in the history of modern architecture (from Crystal Palace (1851) via Berlage's Exchange (1903), Gropius' Fagus-Werke (1912) and Rietveld's Schröder House (1924) to Mies van der Rohe's grid-skyscrapers in Chicago). But at the same time they claim that this group, which made its mark on the journal *Architectura*, 'was the artistic conscience of the architect, who became more and more of an entrepreneur and engineer, thereby losing much of his creativity'. A typical example of this role as 'keeper of the conscience' is the criticism levelled at Berlage's Exchange by De Bazel, Bauer and Walenkamp. Lauweriks speaks of its 'trendy sobriety and forced simplicity', De Bazel of its profit motivation: 'art should not, however, resign itself to this, but must fight towards developing a better insight into the conditions and relations needed to bring about a genuine monumentality'.

There is an added piquancy in that there were frequent points of contact between these gentlemen and that their views on one another's work were expressed, not only in letters, friendly or otherwise, but also in reviews which, naturally, could influence sponsors, and, more importantly, in jury reports and at committee meetings. A numer of the buildings mentioned in this book remained unbuilt because architect colleagues exercised their veto. That they studied each other's work very closely is evident, for instance, from

M. de Klerk, competition design for a club house in a sports field, motto 'The Fourth', 1907.

M. de Klerk, competition design for a water tower with service buildings, in reinforced concrete, 1912.

M. de Klerk, competition design for a café-restaurant, motto 'Monoliet', 1907.

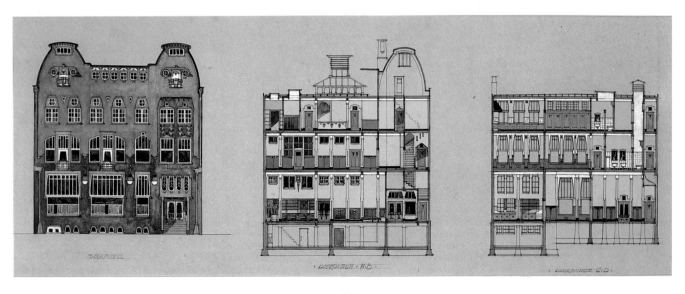

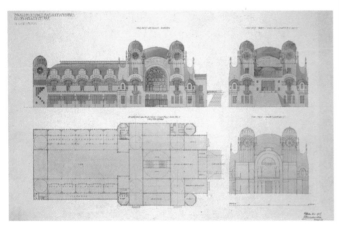

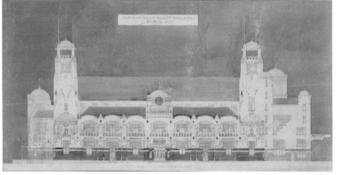

W. Kromhout, first and second designs for the Dutch pavilion at the world exhibition in Brussels, 1908-1910.

The Dutch business world wanted to create a good impression at the world exhibition in Brussels and asked Kromhout as early as 1908 to design its own pavilion. Kromhout's design was 'conceived entirely in iron, monier (a kind of reinformed concrete) and glass, a very modern exhibition building'. (Kromhout in Architectura, 18, 1910, page 234). However, Parliament rejected the design because the construction costs of six hundred thousand guilders were considered too high.
The industrialists did not give up, and invited Kromhout to make a simpler design. Kromhout set to

work again and submitted a design using cheaper materials. 'This design includes a tall brick base with the rest of the structure to be stucco, later to be finished in polychrome' (idem). Kromhout seemed pleased with his design, for he remarked: 'Looked at in this way, I think being asked to design a modern exhibition building is a fine thing'. (idem).

the fact that Berlage — one of three jury members — rejects the competition design for a public library in 1895. One of his reasons: 'dubious monumentality', and another: 'strange, here and there indented ornamentation reminiscent of wood carving'. This does not prevent Berlage, who, in his design for a vestibule for a royal residence (1885) does not himself shun a sumptuous, voluptuous style, from using a number of De Bazel's rejected ideas for his Exchange. which in its turn was criticized by De Bazel.

In 1898 Berlage finally turned away from all that was Art Nouveau. The breach between momumental community art and hyper-individualism becomes clear. 'The ambiguity', says Jan Romein (*Op het*

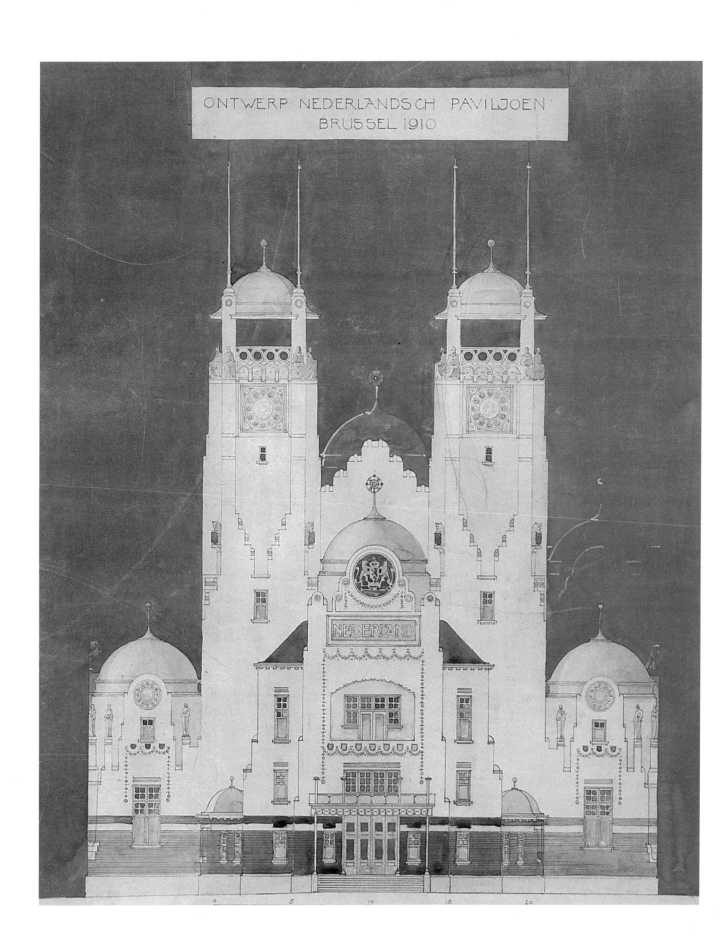

ONTWERP NEDERLANDSCH PAVILJOEN
BRUSSEL 1910

However, the Dutch Commission for the World Exhibition then invited Kromhout to make another draft outline for a pavilion, this time in traditional Dutch style. This draft was immediately accepted.

On the floorplan of his second design Kromhout was then asked to erect a building with stepped gables. His pavilion was thus 'transformed from a modern aristocrat, as it had been in conception, into some sort of Spanish Brabander'. In self-mockery he adds: 'Architecture isn't so difficult'. (idem).

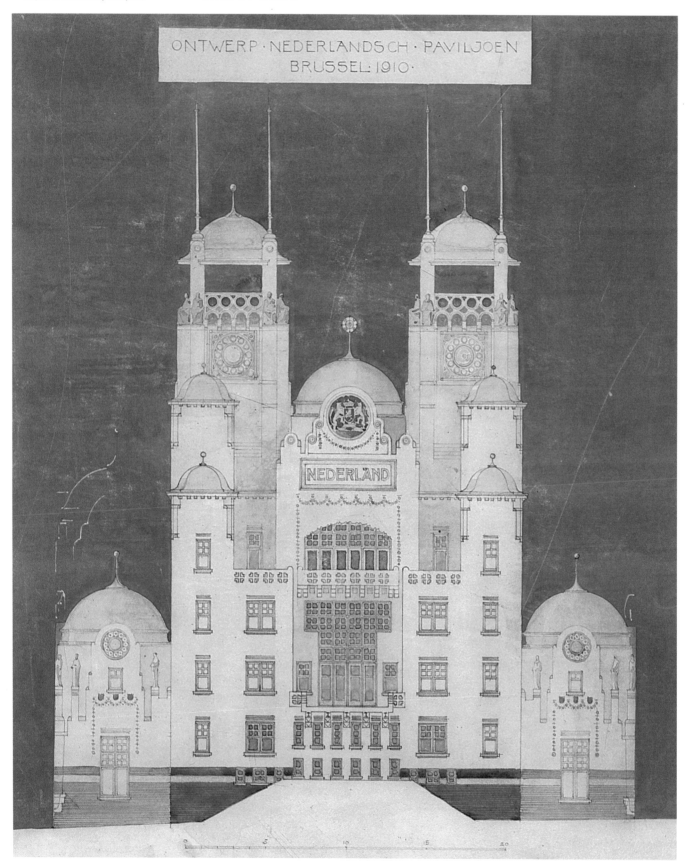

ONTWERP · NEDERLANDSCH · PAVILJOEN
BRUSSEL: 1910 ·

NEDERLAND

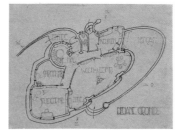 

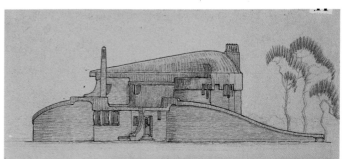

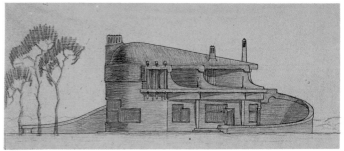

breukvlak van twee eeuwen, Querido) 'of the Art Nouveau style in the Netherlands has been eliminated by the elimination of the style itself. But this has not solved the ambiguity as such. The community art of which the monumentalists dreamt around the turn of the century, has not come. They were unable to overcome the ambiguity of the transitional period in which they lived. Dream and deed are hostile twins.'

Thus the sober but prosperous trading nation in the marshy delta remained deprived of the monumental constructions assembled in the first section of this book. The dreams stayed on paper. Lodewijk van Deyssel proclaimed the eighteen eighties as a new Golden Age, but its architectural counterpart was never realized. What remains are the documents, letters, journals and designs, the idealism faded on paper, of a generation that was busy liberating itself from the hypocritical corsets of Victorian morality, a generation that had recognized the evil side effects of industrialization and the stupefying power of materialism, and that worshipped Beauty in a country always preoccupied with other things.

In 1980 the shops are full of Art Nouveau again, facsimile reprints of the poets of the eighteen eighties are doing well in the book trade. God knows how we would have cherished those buoldings if they had been there. But they are not.

A. Eibink and J.A. Snellebrand, design for a country house in the dunes, 1917.

M. de Klerk, design for a housing complex in a small provincial town, 1915.

A. Eibink and J.A. Snellebrand, competition design for a Dutch Reformed Church in Elshout, motto 'Leo, the burning heart of the World', 1916.

For the competition for a small church in Elshout, architects Eibink and Snellebrand submitted a remarkable design. Here, for the first time, concrete was used as a means towards creating a structure that seemed to have been cast into a single mould: organic architecture. The jury was unable to muster much enthusiasm: 'The jury feels it has to regard this design as an expression of an inflated imagination which has not, however, in any respect solved the question of designing a simple village church. Whatever merit this design may possess in itself, it would not be appropriate in the given setting, even leaving aside the fact that the practical obstacles would be very considerable and that the construction costs would far exceed the stipulated sum'. (Architectura, 25, 1917, page 16).

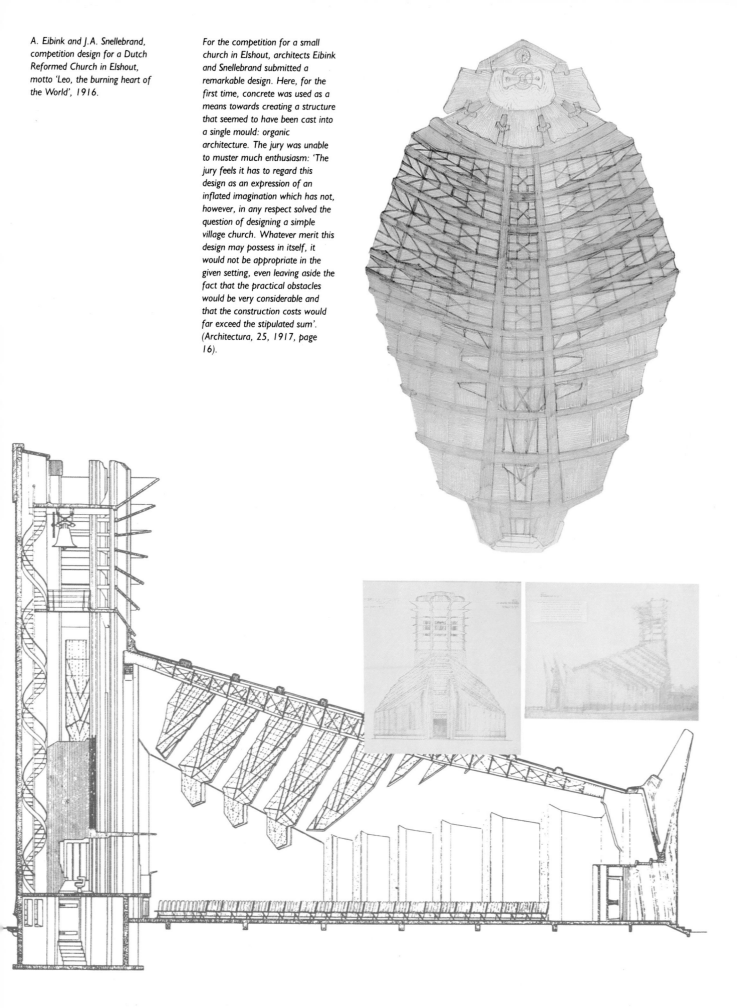

J.L.M. Lauweriks, design for a world war memorial, 1915.

During the first world war, Lauweriks, who had been working in the German town of Hagen since 1909, designed a monument to the dead, which looked similar in conception to Berlage's Pantheon of Mankind. However, while Berlage made his monument into a great temple, Lauweriks designed a park four kilometres long, entirely based on a mathematical plan. In the park, which is situated by a river or lake, there are a triumphal arch, an openair theatre, sculptures and altars, a pantheon and a museum, amid gardens and ponds. On a spur of land running into the water stand a sacred building and an altar. In contrast to Berlage's design, which is intended to be a place of reflection on the horrors of war, Lauweriks' monument clearly has a religious and cultural significance: a sanctuary surrounded by a wall and a moat, from which the harsh world would be excluded.

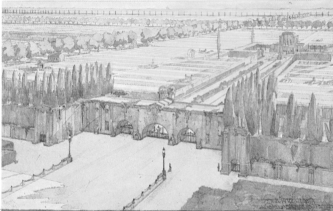

M. de Klerk. Competition design for a public cemetery, motto: 'Reincarnation', 1910.

'O to be free and to be able
To stand each hour on the edge of
the earth
And gaze into the Universe, a free,
free man'.
(Herman Gorter, used by Berlage
as the motto for his design).

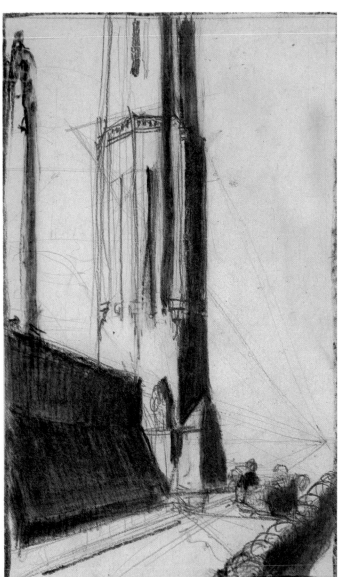

H.P. Berlage, design for a
Pantheon of Mankind, 1915.

Berlage designed the Pantheon of
Mankind during the first world war
with the intention of building it
somewhere in Europe after the
war, as a symbol of the unity of all
peoples and as a monument to the
dead of all countries involved in the
war.
The groundplan of the Pantheon
was inspired by the plans for the
ideal city from the Renaissance;
the structure – a dome-topped
building surrounded by towers – is
related to the mosque.
'Eight highroads lead from all the
points of the compass to the
entrances. These, situated between
the towers of love and courage, of
inspiration and contemplation, of
knowledge and power and of
freedom and peace, that stand as
guardians around the large hall,
radiating their light far and wide at
night, give access to the pantheon.
On either side are gardens for
meditation, enclosed by the

galleries for the commemoration of
the dead of the warring states.
Through the galleries of
reconciliation, the great hall is
reached. There, enclosed by the
gallery of memory, lit only by the
zenith light from the cupola,
stands the monument to the unity
of mankind. Higher up, the
galleries of recognition, of
exaltation and of all-
encompassment are reached, and
the structure is closed at the top by
the dome of the community of
nations'. (from: H.P. Berlage, The
Pantheon of Mankind, Pictures of
the designs, with legends in verse
by Henriette Roland Holst-Van der
Schalk, Rotterdam, 1919).

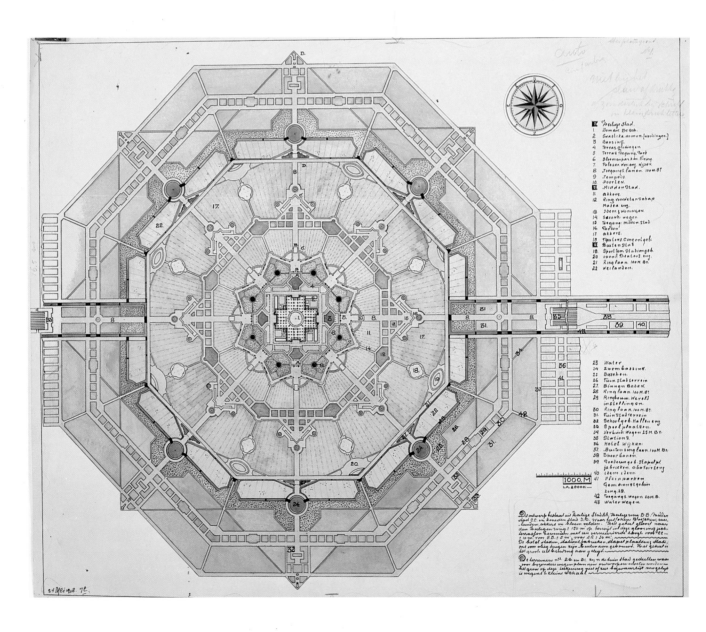

J. London, design for a 'City of Light', 1921.

'We are going to build the house of God in the City of Light. The sacred centre of all humankind, from which every activity of all human beings inhabitant of this planet, this Earth, this flying home of our species, is governed, organized and sanctified. A great temple we shall build, as great and beautiful as human strength allows. A worldhouse, not to the glory of man but to the glory of God, the strongest expression in form, line and colour, of man's striving to become one with the Almighty who has sent us into combat and is awaiting us, in the ultimate triumph'.

With these words Frederik van Eeden introduces, in his book 'The House of God in the City of Light' in 1921, his plans for the foundation of an ideal state – the City of Light – for which J. London designed the architecture. The plan can be compared with De Bazel's World Capital, Lauweriks' World war memorial and Berlage's Pantheon of Mankind, with the difference that Van Eeden's concept has a strongly religious character. It is the utopia that unites them; they are all a plea for the unity and brotherhood of nations and at the same time a monument to the horrors of the first world war.
The City of Light was to be founded on an island, surrounded by water on all sides; hallowed

Delphi was to Hellas and Mecca is to Islam, the great Temple of Brotherhood and the City of Light built around it will be to all mankind'.

In his last chapter, 'The Task of the Invisible Appeal', Van Eeden concludes his plea as follows: 'So the City of Light, which strives for equilibrium, will be the first harmoniously happy city of man. With this in mind, I must

ground, screened from all corruption. It was to be an independent, sovereign state, in which all worldly powers would be represented. Van Eeden compares the City of Light with ancient Hellas, where Delphi was a hallowed place of assembly and a centre of Hellenic culture: 'What

concluded that the City of Light is not a utopia, not an unrealizable ideal, but that it is demanded by our human condition.
It is the task of this great twentieth century to carry it out; as unparalleled in its splendour as the war was unparalleled in its horror'.

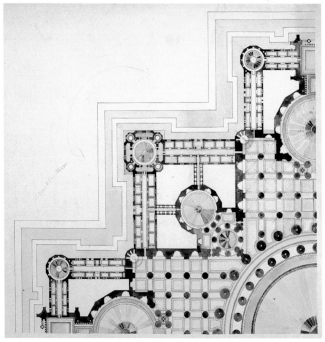

The city is a people's art, a shared experience, the place where the artist meets the greatest number of potential appreciators.

J.C. van Epen, artist's impressions of skyscrapers, ± 1920.

Van Epen's skyscrapers are related to the work of German expressionist architects from the same period. They suggest that he was familiar with Bruno Taut's ideas on 'architecture as luminous crystal, a symbol of a new society'. Taut set forth his ideas in books such as 'Die Stadtkrone' and 'Alpine Architektur' and especially in the journal 'Frühlicht', in which he published his correspondence with friends, including Finterlin, Gropius, Scharoun and the Luckhardt brothers.

'... Transparent and bright, a new world lights up in spring, it sends out its first rays.... And the golden orb of architecture, of art generally, begins its triumphant course'. (Frühlicht, 1921, nr. 1, Autumn).

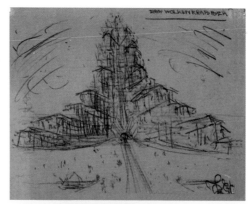

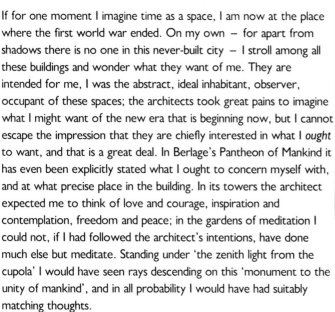

If for one moment I imagine time as a space, I am now at the place where the first world war ended. On my own — for apart from shadows there is no one in this never-built city — I stroll among all these buildings and wonder what they want of me. They are intended for me, I was the abstract, ideal inhabitant, observer, occupant of these spaces; the architects took great pains to imagine what I might want of the new era that is beginning now, but I cannot escape the impression that they are chiefly interested in what I *ought* to want, and that is a great deal. In Berlage's Pantheon of Mankind it has even been explicitly stated what I ought to concern myself with, and at what precise place in the building. In its towers the architect expected me to think of love and courage, inspiration and contemplation, freedom and peace; in the gardens of meditation I could not, if I had followed the architect's intentions, have done much else but meditate. Standing under 'the zenith light from the cupola' I would have seen rays descending on this 'monument to the unity of mankind', and in all probability I would have had suitably matching thoughts.

What kind of person would I then have been? This is no mere

J. Duiker and B. Bijvoet, competition design for the State Academy of Art, Amsterdam, 1917-1918.

In 1917 the Dutch government organized a competition for a State Academy of Arts and Design. Something very special is expected of a building for the most advanced form of art teaching. In its introduction to the rules for the competition, the jury remarked: 'The building will have to meet the requirements of the Academy in such a way, and it will therefore have to be designed in such a way, that both in its totality and in its detail it will, as far as possible, deserve to be called a work of art. Its aesthetic form must express in particular that the building is intended for the advanced teaching of the arts of design'.
The competition consisted of two rounds.
On 22 Februari 1918 the final decision was taken. Without a roll-call vote, the design under motto 'VI' by Duiker and Bijvoet was awarded first prize and the design under motto 'Great Amsterdam' by De Klerk received the second prize. That the decision of the jury was not as unanimous as would appear from its report, is demonstrated by a letter from R.N. Roland Holst to Wijdeveld (dated 24-2-18, coll NDB) 'I don't have to make a secret of it that I too would have preferred to give the first prize to De Klerk and that

I remained loyal to him to the end, although I am only too well aware of De Klerk's weaknesses, beside his brilliant qualities'.
Eventually, the commission given to Duiker and Bijvoet is withdrawn owing to lack of funds.

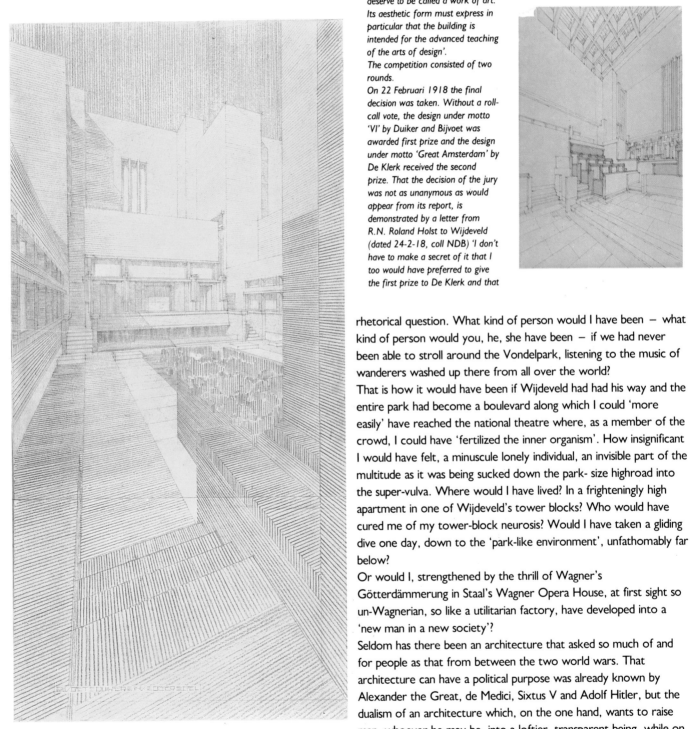

rhetorical question. What kind of person would I have been – what kind of person would you, he, she have been – if we had never been able to stroll around the Vondelpark, listening to the music of wanderers washed up there from all over the world?
That is how it would have been if Wijdeveld had had his way and the entire park had become a boulevard along which I could 'more easily' have reached the national theatre where, as a member of the crowd, I could have 'fertilized the inner organism'. How insignificant I would have felt, a minuscule lonely individual, an invisible part of the multitude as it was being sucked down the park-size highroad into the super-vulva. Where would I have lived? In a frighteningly high apartment in one of Wijdeveld's tower blocks? Who would have cured me of my tower-block neurosis? Would I have taken a gliding dive one day, down to the 'park-like environment', unfathomably far below?
Or would I, strengthened by the thrill of Wagner's Götterdämmerung in Staal's Wagner Opera House, at first sight so un-Wagnerian, so like a utilitarian factory, have developed into a 'new man in a new society'?
Seldom has there been an architecture that asked so much of and for people as that from between the two world wars. That architecture can have a political purpose was already known by Alexander the Great, de Medici, Sixtus V and Adolf Hitler, but the dualism of an architecture which, on the one hand, wants to raise man, whoever he may be, into a loftier, transparent being, while on the other hand it is intended to confirm him in his role of participant in the production process is new.

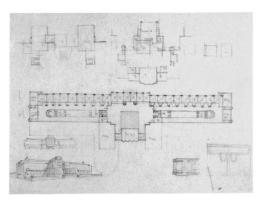

What do we ask of cities? 'From my earliest childhood', writes Harry Mulisch in *De Toekomst van Gisteren*, 'I have dreamt intermittently of a city. Although in the dream itself there is no real, concrete indication of it, this city is filled with bliss; the gigantic black façades, the wide streets, the light, the noise, the night, the *museum*, everything is bliss, and this bliss continues even for a long time after waking. It is impossible to say why this is so: I must think of something to describe it — for instance: death does not exist in that city. Its ultimate source lies almost certainly in a prenatal awareness, in a memory of my existence in the womb, — but why should that have taken the form of a city?'

The same dream, that of an immortal life within the embrace of a city, is described by a very different and much earlier writer —

42

*J.J.P. Oud, design for a factory
with offices and warehouses
Purmerend, 1919.*

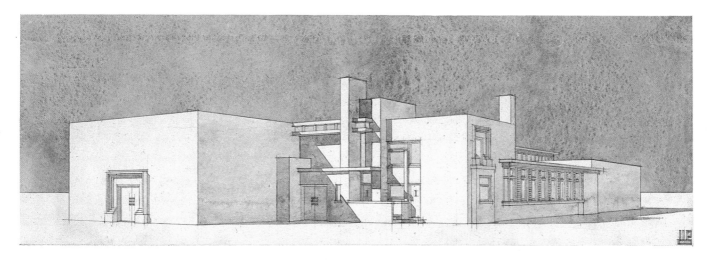

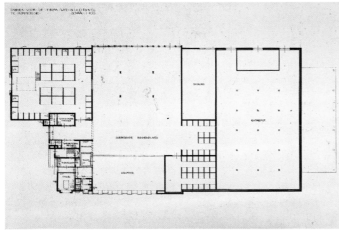

About the factory he designed for his family's wine and spirits business, Oud says himself: in 'My way in De Stijl' (The Hague-Rotterdam, 1957-1958, p. 17-18):

'In the year 1919 I attempted, in a design for a factory, to achieve in three dimensions what Mondriaan had realized in his paintings, in two dimensions. The contrast between lines and coloured areas I translated into architecture by placing open opposite closed, glass opposite wall. I tried to make this contrast into a modern, independent construction -element, and transformed Mondriaan's tension between horizontals and verticals into horizontal-vertical construction units, thereby extending the idea into the three-

*dimensional sphere'....
'The language of the design itself gradually began to mean less to me, as did its spirit, when I had tried, in several buildings, to realize this somehow unworldly aesthetic on the basis of a normal construction procedure, i.e. without forcing the function and the construction of the building too much into the strait-jacket of a predetermined form'.*

Augustine of Hippo, in *De Civitate Dei* (472). The difference is that his city can be conquered only after the experience of Vale of Tears and Death. So there first has to be birth. The City of God, the round, walled city which will protect us like a womb, from which we need never depart again, a house for all eternity. That is one conception of the city. But there are others.

'Man has built and loved cities because in the urban form he constructs the superimage of his ideal self. The common denominator of cities, from Nineveh to New York, is a collective idol worship, praying for power over nature, destiny, knowledge, and wealth.' (Sybil Moholy-Nagy, *Matrix of Man*).

The city as womb, the city as an altar for self-worship, the city as production organism (see Tafuri), the city as a labyrinth in which disorientation is consciously aspired to. (Constant).

Roving through all those imaginary cities I wander in the direction of my own city. Part of the year, I am a traveller by profession. For the first time I understand, while studying this city of unbuilt buildings, that I have allowed myself to be manipulated. I knew what I wanted of cities, but what those cities wanted of me I simply allowed to happen. I am the perfect inhabitant.

My first memory of a city is that of a title. During the war, I saw a film, 'The Golden City'. Even in front of a firing squad I would not be able to say more about it than that a blonde woman played in it who excited me immensely, and that it contained pictures of a city in the distance, of which I now know it must have been Prague. Perhaps it was at moments like this that my wanderlust and my hunger for cities were awakened, perhaps I identify cities with women, at all events it is certain that I experience big cities in an erotic sense. There is something exciting about large multitudes and merging into them, and large multitudes are naturally most easily

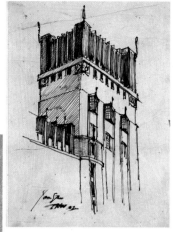

found in big cities.

I am in no doubt that this excitement has something to do with anonymity and with chance, and anonymity and chance are also characteristics of big cities.

He who travels widely has seen the city in all its manifestations; as theatre, as barracks, as living-room, as power centre, as battlefield, as refuge, as museum, as mother and as monster. I have fulfilled my function as part of crowd, as passer-by, in at least a hundred cities. I have let myself be conducted by Haussmann along the boulevards of 1968 Paris, I stood on the charred streets of Budapest in 1956, I fled from police tear gas across the squares of Athens in 1967, I was swept along the Via della Conziliazione in to the arms of Bernini, right under the balcony of St.-Peter's, to see the white, birdlike figure of Pius XII dancing above the heads of the faithful in 1953, I stood with my cardboard periscope on the Dam, at the abdication of Queen Wilhelmina in 1948, I have roamed among the ruins of Persepolis and Ayuthya, where history has melted the inhabitants away, I did not die in Isfahan, I have seen Rotterdam burn and I live in Amsterdam.

But my most precious memory is of Salamanca, and it is worth analysing this, because it tells me on the one hand what I want of cities and on the other hand, how and when this coincides with what

a city wants of me. It was in 1954 and I was hitch-hiking through Spain. The 'discovery' of Spain made a shattering impression on me. Somewhere in my soul there must be a landscape that corresponds with those bare-battered, in those days still much emptier' deserts of the Spanish plateau in which, every so many hundred kilometres, a city looms up. The word 'loom' is no coincidence; there is something of doom and apparition in the sight of a city when it becomes visible from a distance. You are driven towards it as though prodded in the back by a divine finger, and this driving force continues even within the walls − in such cities you find the centre without a moment's hesitation.

In the case of Salamanca this is the Plaza Mayor. I took simple lodgings on the South side of the square and sat in the window of my room with a drink, when suddenly, at around eight o'clock, the square totally changed in appearance. Before that moment it had been beautiful enough: a quadrangle without sidewalks or raised areas, surrounded on all sides by one single building resting on four long colonnades. In fact, the square was a large stone room with the sky as its ceiling. People moved more or less randomly from North to South and from East to West; they emerged from shops under the colonnades or from one of the narrow streets leading into the square, but at that indefinable moment the whole scene changed. As if it were a matter of course, a circle was formed within the square,

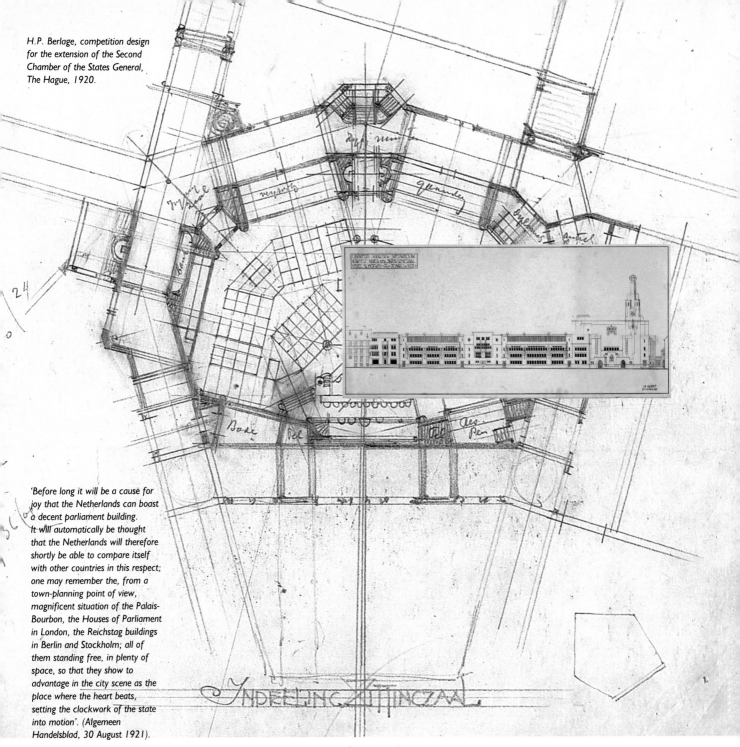

H.P. Berlage, competition design for the extension of the Second Chamber of the States General, The Hague, 1920.

'Before long it will be a cause for joy that the Netherlands can boast a decent parliament building. It will automatically be thought that the Netherlands will therefore shortly be able to compare itself with other countries in this respect; one may remember the, from a town-planning point of view, magnificent situation of the Palais-Bourbon, the Houses of Parliament in London, the Reichstag buildings in Berlin and Stockholm; all of them standing free, in plenty of space, so that they show to advantage in the city scene as the place where the heart beats, setting the clockwork of the state into motion'. (Algemeen Handelsblad, 30 August 1921).

As it happened, the task of designing a suitably monumental new building in a historic environment was beset with difficulties. The site for the future parliament building lay alongside relatively narrow streets, which moreover taper off into a sharp point, and the competition programm specified that the existing Binnenhof façades would have to be preserved. None of the candidates proved able to design a satisfactory solution and the competiton was considered to have been a failure.

H. Th. Wijdeveld, design for high-
rise buildings in parkland
surroundings, 1919-1922.

a walking — to be precise: a backward-and-forward walking circle of living people, which slowly began to rotate.

In some way or other I knew: this is what the world ought to look like. I sat by my window, in a stunned state, consumed by a longing to be allowed to join in. But if this was what the world ought to look like, there would first have to be cities with squares such as this, and these squares would have to be exactly in the city centres. On my travels I am usually a loner, but at that moment I was profoundly moved by the vision of the completely natural, communal spirit of that crowd down below.

Those people were doing this because the square asked it of them, perhaps even demanded it. But they would never have done it if they had not *wanted* to. In many Latin cities the street, the café, the square, the river bank, form the natural extension of the home. After work, people assemble, watching each other and talking. But in other cities there is always a possibility of escape, there is a self-

selected moment when the paseo (stroll) turns round at a given street corner. I have never seen so forcibly the inescapability of genuine social contact as in that revolving human circle in that square of age-old stone. It was a peaceful sight, but Spain, and also this square, had know other crowds in other moods.

However, a crowd in whatever mood remains a crowd, whether it has gathered to celebrate its freedom, whether it wants to — or is forced to — cheer its leader, or set fire to his Palace. No one has put this into words better than Elias Canetti when in *Die Fackel im Ohr* (Hanser, 1980) he described himself as part of the crowd that set fire to the palace of Justice in Vienna — in 1927, after a verdict that the people regarded as unjust:

'I cannot see myself clearly on this day but I still *feel* the excitement, the running forward, the evasive action, the flowing movement... (I)... was for the first time at the mercy of the masses, unable to resist. Since then I have always remembered how gladly one

H.Th. Wijdeveld, Vondelpark project with Large National Theatre, Amsterdam, 1919.

To Wijdeveld, high-rise meant a means to create order in the chaos of ever-expanding, densely built cities. He considered the Vondelpark in Amsterdam as an obstacle that should be transformed into a boulevard along which there would be high-rise buildings for government offices, bordered by gardens that would be the only relics of the park.
According to Wijdeveld, parks had for too long been regarded as the lungs of the city, and would now have to grow with the 'metropolitan body' and be turned into traffic arteries.
In order to make this fairly dangerous idea acceptable to the public, Wijdeveld envisaged a national theatre at one end of the

park. Everyone has, after all, 'the right to immediate participation in and enjoyment of the culture of his time' (Wendingen 1919, nr. 9-10 p. 7). The great boulevard is therefore not so much intended for motorized traffic as to make it easier for people to gain access to the theatre!... 'We see it as the great watchman at the end of the great boulevard, inviting approach by means of its massive, towering structure, offering access through great curved entrances, while the tall doors, opening wide, call upon the multitudes as they come pouring in, to fertilize its inner organism' (idem, p. 9).

surrenders to the masses. I saw masses around me, but I saw also masses within me, and I was unable to give a clear-cut explanation. In Freud's treatise (*Massenpsychologie und Ich-analyse* – Mass Psychology and the Analysis of the I) I missed most of all the acknowledgment of this phenomenon. It seemed to me no less elementary than libido and hunger.'

I quote this at such length because twentieth century architecture was to occupy itself so extensively and in so many ways with the problem of the masses. The masses were there and would, it was thought, continue to increase. They would have to be accommodated, they would have to be able to function, they would have to be amused, taught, and, if possible, elevated to a higher level; they would, literally, need space, and architecture had to provide this space, divide it, organize it and manipulate it. There has never been more and loftier philosophical talk about the role of architecture in our society than there was at the beginning of this century.

Architects saw themselves as artists, as community philosophers, as the blessed creators of a New World. It is sometimes difficult to remember that they knew only too well they had to build this New World among the remains of the old. The tone they adopt has something godlike about it – it seems as if it is they who are also going to create the crowds of human beings who will populate their buildings. The *actual* crowds of their time, the people they saw in the street or in the trams, will not at all, or hardly, have resembled the 'high idea' they had of *their* crowds. Of course this is not true of all the architects of that time, but the tone is unmistakable. It is probably unavoidable too.

Even if the influence of architecture – in the widest sense, and therefore with the inclusion of town-planning – on the daily lives of 'the people' is not as great as *I* think it is, then the person who is entrusted with the task to build – in principle – for all the others, will still find it difficult not to adopt a certain superhuman stance.

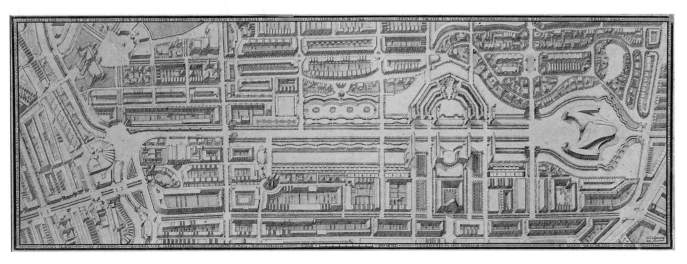

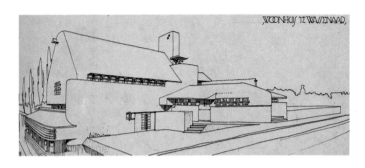

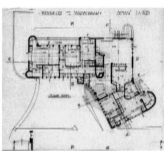

M. de Klerk, design for a villa in
Wasselaar, 1923.

Bruno Taut, the leader of the Glaskette designers' group in Berlin, proposed to turn an Alpine peak into a symbolic crystal city which would have to serve as inspiration to the builders of a new urban world 'in which man and earth would be each other's complement'. One of his glass community centres (he wanted to abolish the distinction between public buildings and private dwellings) contained, among other things, the following components: areas for agricultural exhibitions and experiments... an arena for performances... rows of seats on those levels where the hotels (!) are situated... a canal... a crane to lift grain into the granaries, to be stored for the lean years... facilities for arrival and departure by water, land and air... amusement park...'

The architect as the creator of a cosmos. It must have been a wonderful feeling. His friend, the architect Herman Finsterlin, put it perhaps even more clearly. He wanted to continue God's creation where it had been left off on the seventh day. He tried in his designs to achieve a continuity between landscape, garden, house and furniture.

Rudolf Steiner was interested in the moral influence of architecture, and therefore especially in the forms it took. He strove towards an architecture inspired by nature, representing an organic whole. To all these architects it went without saying that an architecture linked to nature would be enriched by this new spirituality. And once again the godlike stance makes its appearance, when the phrase 'cathedrals of the future' is uttered.

A good example of the architect as 'divine' artist can be found in an anecdote about Erich Mendelsohn, the designer of the famous Einstein Tower, an observatory in Potsdam, one of the most fantastical buildings of the first quarter of this century. He liked to work to music – as his name would suggest – and had a preference fo the clear, mathematical compositions of Bach. Patrons who knew this, asked him to design a building to the music of Brahms, but he replied that the music served only to create the right atmosphere in which his imagination could best develop.

But perhaps Berlage, in his *Beschouwingen over Stijl*, shows more clearly than anyone the problems with which the architect-artist struggled at the beginning of the century: The phrase 'Artist, don't talk – create!' still remains true. And among the true philosophers there seems to be a difference of opinion, so much so that the great thinkers cannot even make up their minds about the artistry of architecture, that is to say, about the question whether or not it is art at all.

One needs only to read Kant, Schopenhauer, Solger, Krause, Hegel, Trahndorff, Weisze and others on this point to find proof of how difficult it is to define what architecture is, and naturally, when a further question is asked, about the 'how', this is even more difficult to answer. This is again understandable, because philosophers are not performing artists. And as it is still true that 'All theory is grey and only the golden tree of life is green', no scholar has yet been able to teach a Beethoven or a Wagner how to compose, nor a Praxiteles and a Michelangelo how to sculpt; no philosopher has succeeded in teaching a Raphael and a Rembrandt how to paint or an Iktinos or a Bramante how to build. Yes, even a Ruskin, who is sometimes called the father of modern art, remains a scholar from whom artists can learn little to help them with their actual work. And once again, it is clear why this is so. For philosophy can only draw conclusions from phenomena; it can, at a pinch, analyse people's ideas in advance, but it can definitely not prescribe art. No, then those great practical artists like Viollet-le-Duc in France and the already mentioned Semper in Germany, to name but two of the highly talented people who, moreover, were also capable of recording their reflections on art, were better teachers, for in their great works, *le Dictionnaire*

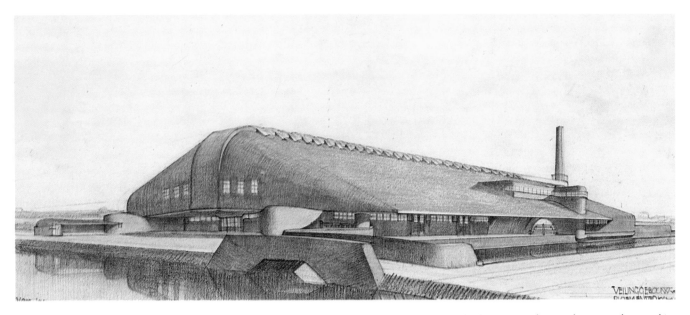

raisonné de l'architecture and *Der Stil in den Technischen Kunsten* they offer a practical system of aesthetics, one that can be used, and according to which one can work. For what is it all about? Nothing more or less than style. Not only a kingdom, but Heaven for a style! is the desperate cry. That is the great happiness we have lost. We must fight against sham art. We want, once again, the essence, not the appearance. The essence of architecture! That is the truth and once again the truth, which we pursue, for even in art, lies have become the rule, truth the exception. That is why architects must try once again to get at the truth, that is, to understand the essence of architecture.

Now architecture is and remains the art of construction, that is to say, the art of the composition of various elements, the organization of space, and because this basic principle is no longer understood in its full meaning, we must strive towards good, that is pure, construction, boldly carried out, in the simplest form.' (*Studies over bouwkunst, stijl en samenleving*, W.L. & J. Brusse, publishers, Rotterdam, 1910).

'To get at the truth... to understand the essence of architecture'. But which essence, and which architecture? What the next thirty years have to show, looks more like an explosion than anything else. The answers given to the problems are of a bewildering complexity and they come from both home and abroad. They intersect, they cross-influence each other, oppose each other, and the layman who, forty years later, tries to find his way around this multiplicity of propositions, theories, polemics, and the reflections thereof in built and unbuilt cities, needs a chopping knife and an infallible compass so as not to get lost in the jungle of ideas.

Sometimes it is as though you were reading church history, with dogmas, dissensions, heresies, schisms, denunciations, apostasies, prophesies — with saints and devils, patriarchs and excommunications. Time and again, preachers and thinkers nail a new doctrine to the church doors, the stakes are immense, and

C. van Eesteren, design for Maison Particulière, in collaboration with Theo van Doesburg (for the colour), 1923.

In 1922 van Eesteren met Theo van Doesburg, the founder and driving force of the journal 'De Stijl' and the group around it, which included, in the initial period, the painter Mondriaan and the architects Oud and Wils. In 1923 he had a number of projects in hand (a house for the art dealer Leonce Rosenberg, the maison particulière and the maison d'artiste): these last two, insofar as the colours are concerned, in collaboration with Van Doesburg. This collaboration inaugurates a new phase of De Stijl architecture, in which the systematic exploration of space and form (and colour) is given expression in a manifesto that starts as follows: 'Working collectively, we have examined architecture as a unity, created out of all the arts, industry, technique etc., and we have found that the result will be a new style'. As a vague reflection of this architecture, the Schröder House was built in Utrecht in 1924 by the architect Rietveld. These models have been of enormous importance in the world (chiefly by being the bad conscience of architects).

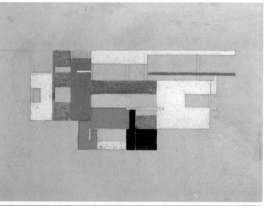

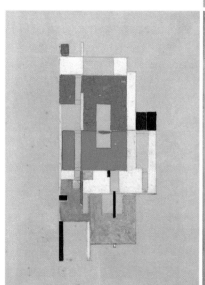

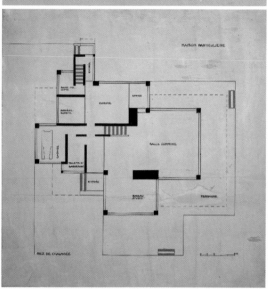

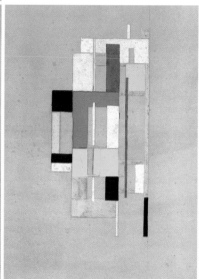

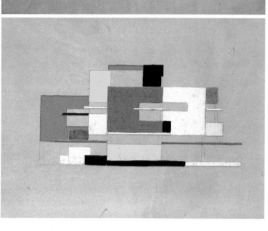

M. Stam, design for a building
plan for the Rokin, Amsterdam,
1926.

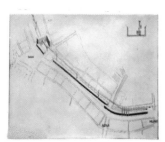

Mart Stam's design for a building
plan for the Rokin was made two
years after the Rokin competition
of 1924, probably as a result of
the unsatisfactory outcome of this
competition. In his plan, Stam
wants to meet in one go a number
of needs that exist in the city at
that moment, namely, the need for
office space, the need for car
parking space, and the need for
good communications with the
suburbs. Stam solves these
problems as follows: By having the
offices built on pylons, space is
released at ground level which can
serve as covered walkway and as
car park; quick transport
throughout the whole city Stam has
made possible by constructing a

'highway' above the offices,
hanging from cables and driven by
a propellor.

Stam himself says of this design:
'The underlying principle of this
attempt to illuminate the Rokin
problem from another angle, was
the need to abandon the rigid
priciple of a 'closed city scene, of
squares with closed sides'. Less
architectural bombast, and
therefore more honesty and
usefulness'. (Het Bouwbedrijf, 4,
1927, p. 18).

The international competition for a Lenin Museum was organized by the Competition Commission of the Central Executive Committee of the USSR to immortalize the memory of V.I. Lenin.

The design, which bears the name of Berlage, was really made by his son-in-law E.E. Strasser and his partner B. Wille, 'under the strong artistic influence of Berlage', as they themselves said in their accompanying statement.
The mausoleum consists of a pyramid like dome with 'two obelisks flanking the tomb like watchmen'. From the crystal-like decoration at the top of these obelisks, light would shine at night. To the left and right of this central section run two covered corridors parallel with the Kremlin wall. Through these corridors, great streams of visitors can enter the mausoleum from two directions at once. In the mausoleum itself, one corridor lies higher than the other, so that the visitors on both corridors do not get in each other's way.
After viewing, the visitors can leave the mausoleum by the opposite corridor.

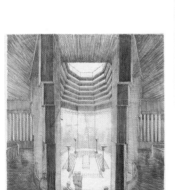

H.P. Berlage, competition design for a mausoleum for Lenin, Moscow, 1926.

especially fascinating because the crux of the matter was and remained (and remains): what is the world going to look like, or what ought it to look like, and closely related to this, in the view of many of the people involved: what is society like, or what ought it to be like?

It is very fortunate that, during a variety of developments, whether these are concerned with the aesthetic-utopian Amsterdam School or with high-rise building, with the synthesis of the arts or with an international work-community, Wijdeveld never kept his mouth shut.
He is now ninety five years old and leaves a trail of utterances behind him which are still so lively that one is always pleased – and sometimes amused – to see them cropping up in various publications, because they so often offer a surprising insight into the

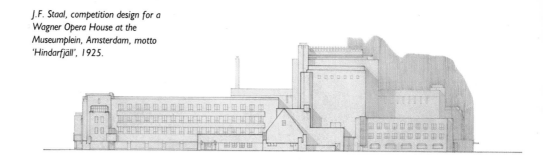

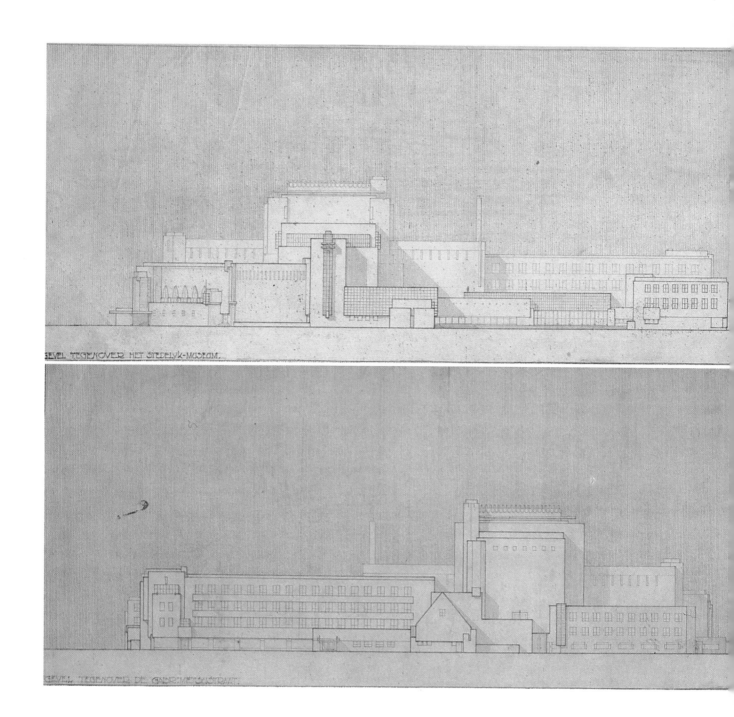

GEVEL TEGENOVER HET STEDELIJK-MUSEUM.

GEVEL TEGENOVER DE GABRIEL METSUSTRAAT.

'Yet the exploitation of forces that lie fallow will not bear fruit if at the same time the interest of those among whom art seeks a response is not aroused. This is the social aspect of the problem and the Wagner Society has devoted equal attention to this aspect'. (records of the Wagner Society, Amsterdam, 1934, p. 12).
In order to promote successfully the above-mentioned interest in Wagner's music, the society intended, in the early 1920's, to found its own theatre which would

'at the same time offer an opportunity to meet, both from a musical and a technical point of view, the demands of a perfect interpretation' (idem). This led to a joint invitation to the architects Blaauw, Gratama, Van der Mey, Slothouwer, Staal and Wijdeveld, to design a music theatre at the Museumplein, opposite the Stedelijk Museum. Staal's entry was generally regarded as the best. The asymmetric positioning, with its axes in the direction of Rijksmuseum, Stedelijk Museum

and Concertgebouw, would 'transform the Museumplein into a great monumental area of the city'. (idem p. 65).
After three years, in January 1929, the Burgomaster and Aldermen of Amsterdam proposed to the City Council to make money available for the building of this theatre. However, the proposal was not accepted. The fear of competition, and the effect it would have on the nearby Concertgebouw, was too great.

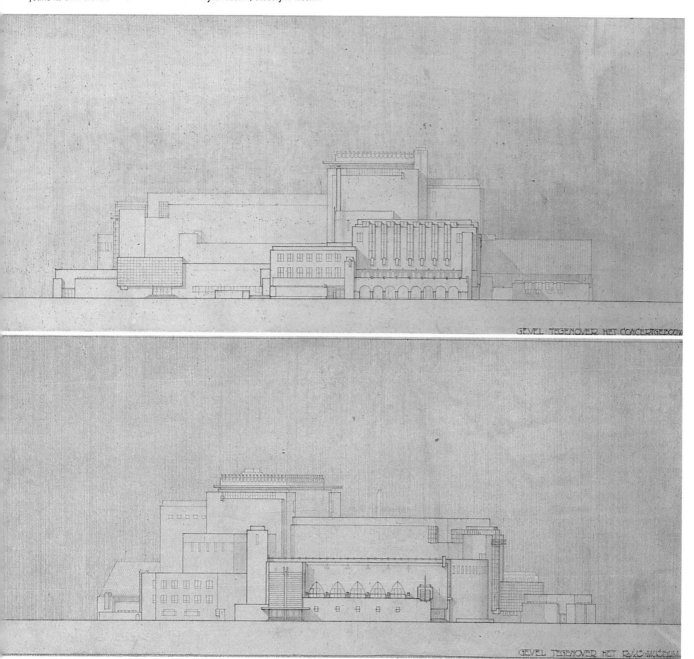

GEVEL TEGENOVER HET CONCERTGEBOUW

GEVEL TEGENOVER HET RIJKSMUSEUM

J.J.P. Oud, competition design for the Exchange in Rotterdam, motto 'X', 1926.

In 1926 a Commission for the Foundation of an Exchange in Rotterdam, set up by the business world, invited six architects to design an exchange at the Coolsingel, next to the post office and the town hall. The architects invited were Granpré Molière, Mertens, Staal, Kromhout, Dudok and Oud. The Rotterdam architectural world was most surprised at this coice, because not one private architect from Rotterdam was included. Oud, who worked for the municipality, was clearly not regarded as a true Rotterdammer. An official protest from the Rotterdam Circle of the BNA persuaded the Exchange Commission to invite two Rotterdam architects' offices, De

Roos & Overeynder and Meischke & Schmidt, to participate in the competition. In July 1927 it was decided to invite architects Staal, Dudok and Mertens for a second round. At the end of 1928, Staal's design was declared the best.
In the introduction to his design, Oud states: 'In front of the aforementioned part of the Exchange at the Coolsingel, additional areas have been projected up to ceiling level, which can be continually re-adapted to any purpose desired (for maximum flexibility of use): shops, department store, café, etc.
It should be remembered that such uses should always contribute to the enlivenment of the rather dull aspect of the Coolsingel at that point with lights, illuminated advertising, etc. Thus, a large café terrace has been planned for this area. The Exchange is not a pet

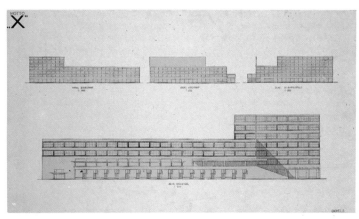

project but a living part of city life. The system of construction is reinforced concrete: beams on columns, centre to centre 5 M (= measure of two dually occupied writing desks). Between these columns the interior arrangement can be easily adjusted – even staircases, lifts etc. – without necessitating any alteration to the exterior appearance. All areas,

even the large Exchange Hall, can be made larger or smaller as desired; office rooms can be installed to the left, right, or on both sides of corridors (windows are identical everywhere)'.
(Bouwkundig Weekblad, 1929, p. 41).
The jury probably considered the whole plan to be too progressive.

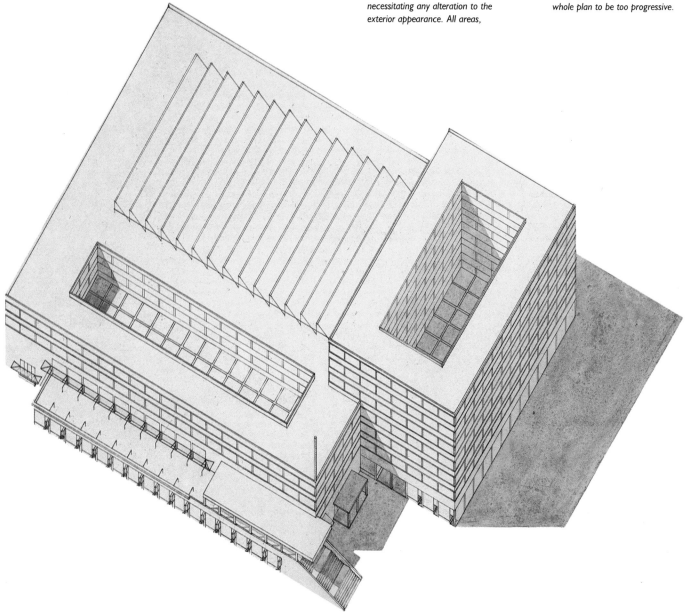

High-rise.
Here again, 'high' ideals.
Beware of petit-bourgeois houses
with front gardens.
Semblance, not essence!
Existing skyscrapers are not very
successful from an economic point
of view.

J. Duiker and J.G. Wiebenga,
1927-1919.

'As for Amsterdam, the land policy
which is intended to transfer the
land to public ownership makes it
possible to plan cities in which
people can not only work but also
live. The attempts recently made
everywhere by townplanners,
doctors, architects etc. to arrive at
satisfactory solutions in this
respect, need no longer remain
purely theoretical, because no
further account need be taken of
the personal interests of big and
small proprietors. Individual
property, a product of history,
which is in some parts of the city
expressed in the shoulder-to-
shoulder building of gentlemen's
houses with separate front and
back gardens, makes a proper
town plan impossible.
It is precisely a social-democracy
that ought to protest against this.
Cries of horror at the first
appearance of high-rise plans, and
the claim that every worker must
have his own little house and
garden in order to be happy, must
be dismissed as thoroughly
bourgeois.
It is the centralized, collective
facilities and amenities that can
raise the standard of living, and
these can never by successfully
realized in a system of so-called
owner-occupation. Everyone knows
that central heating and a centrally
heated water supply are common
items in the programmes of
housing societies. Everyone also
knows in how many cases and at
what price they can be realized.
The case are very few but the price
is usually far too high'.

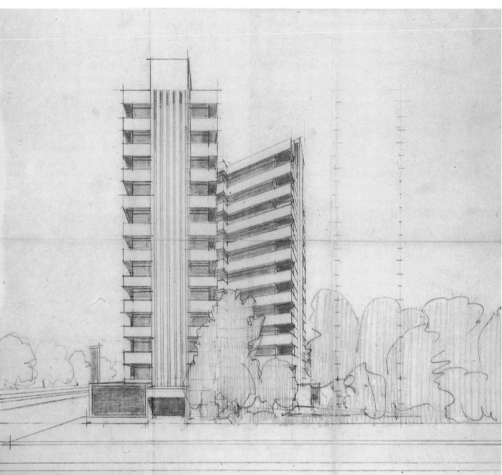

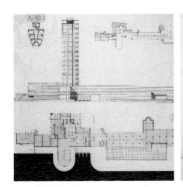
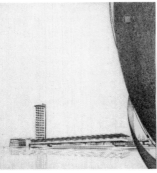

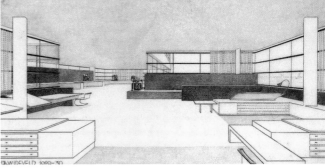

H. Th. Wijdeveld, second design for an International Work Community, Loosdrecht, 1929-1930.

With the Bauhaus in Dessau in mind, Wijdeveld wanted, in the period 1927-1930,. to found a working community by the Loosdrecht Lakes in which architects and designers would be able to work together. In this way the ideal of the medieval guilds would be restored. Students of design would work here under the guidance of experienced architects, they would get practical experience by collaborating with their teachers

on work for which the community had received commissions from industry and the business world. The idea of a working community seems similar to the Bauhaus, and even in the designs for the buildings in which this community was to be established (the first design in 1927, the second in 1927-1930) the Bauhaus example can be easily recognized. The plans were never realized, owing to lack of funds.

issues of the day. Letters to Frank Lloyd Wright, Mendelsohn, Roland Holst, brochures, proclamations and articles in his journal *Wendingen*, never dull, always like the clarion call with which a herald proclaims news to the people. In the Tower House number of *Wendingen* he speaks of the new generation... 'those who, when the End comes, can already feel the tremblings and vibrations of something other, something distant, something New. We feel ourselves to be the builders of a New humanity.'

He is not alone in this. The other architects of the Amsterdam School also think that good art – they still thought of themselves in the first place as individualistic artists – can only arise in a new society. 'The end' of which Wijdeveld speaks must be seen as the end of the old society whose cruel misery, even though the Netherlands had remained outside the world war, had penetrated deeply into the lives of the people. Because of the German and Russian revolutions a social upheaval was expected here too, out of which the new art would have to be born, inspired by a new society in which all people would live together in harmony so that each individual could fulfil his potential to the full and would not be dominated by the few.

The art that would have to develop from this would be a community art, an expression of a higher order of being, and it

would be 'the universal structure or the total image of a spiritual, super-mundane order' as it had been in the Middle Ages.' (W. de Wit, *De architectuur der Amsterdamse School* in: *de Amsterdamse School*, 1975/1979).

Opponents will, of course, not fail to label this as regression, which indeed it is. But within the group itself there is opposition as well. How can community art and individualism be made compatible? 'To the architects of the Amsterdam School, creative action is an expression of the individual, a representation of a private world.' Only by a very intensive exploration of one's own inner mind can one achieve the correct composition, because 'in individualism grows the enchantment of beauty.' (*Wendingen*, 1918, 1)

These ideas become manifest in the three-dimensional composition, in the inspiration based on 'natural' sources, in a strong decorative character which sometimes adds unreal, non-functional elements, in the use of folk-art elements and pre-baked brick, with which all kinds of expressionistic effects can be achieved. Meanwhile, the architects of the Amsterdam School are not without a certain hubris. 'The architect must be allowed to carry out his ideas as he pleases, unhampered either by public opinion or by patrons. The architect-artist knows what is beautiful, and when he offers this beauty to the people by means of his buildings, he will contribute to the uplift of

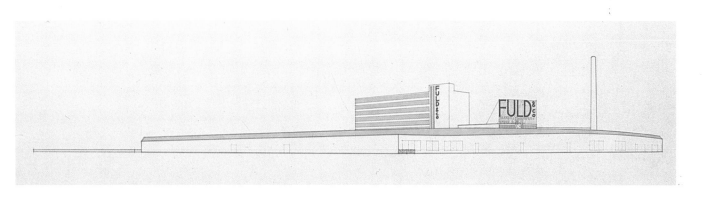

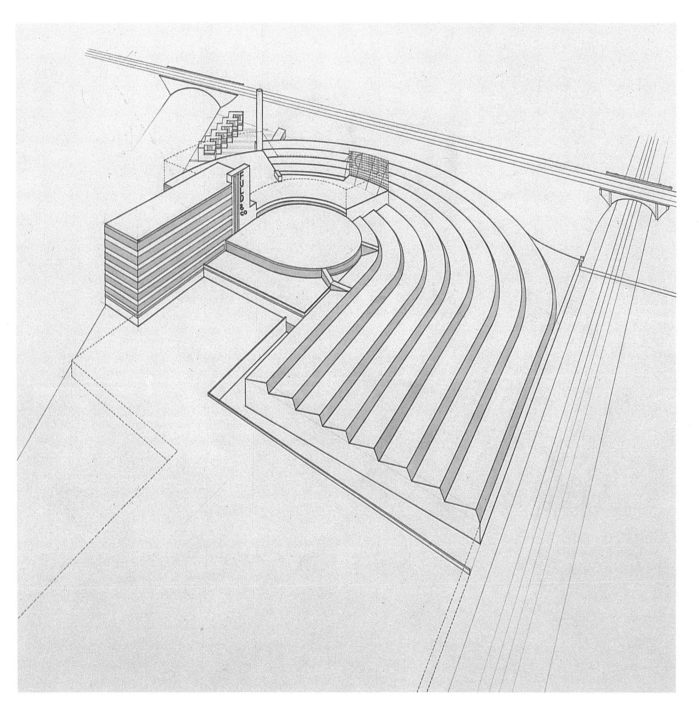

J. Niegeman, competition design
for a factory producing coin-
operated telephones, Fuld & Co,
motto 'Zentral', 1929-1930.

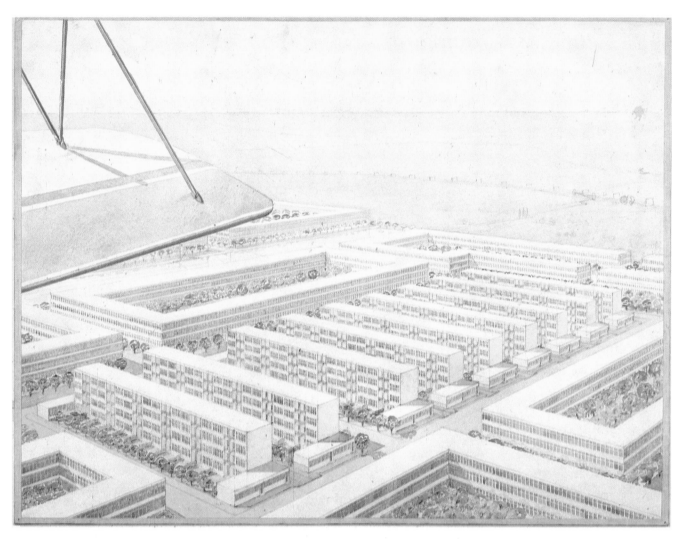

*J.J.P. Oud, design for a housing
estate in Rotterdam-Blijdorp,
1931.*

the people, because someone who lives in a beautiful house will thereby be educated towards beauty, and uplifted to a higher social level.' (W. de Wit, see above).

The fact that 'the people', who had to make do with wretched slum dwellings in the preceding decades, were quite glad to submit to this kind of tutelage, is demonstrated by a remark made by a citizen who says, 'To me it was a shout for joy in stone. I thought: tomorrow everyone will live like this. Then we shall be living in utopia.' (Adriaan Venema, *Sociaal-economische aspecten van de Amsterdamse School*, from: *De Amsterdamse School*, 1975/'79).

That not everyone was equally happy with this art of the 'imaginatives' – the term is again Wijdeveld's ('the imaginatives who play guilelessly with the treasures of rationalism') – soon became clear from the rise of all kinds of groups that blossomed for shorter or longer periods.

The great carnage was over, gaps and ruins recalled an age which, it had been decided, would never be allowed to return, Dada held up a disconcerting distorting mirror to the scandalized bourgeoisie, which horrified most people even more than the horrors of the war had

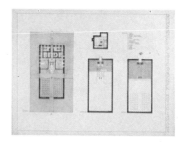

done. Internationalism was the watch-word; ideas darted back and
forth through Europe like shuttles. This had been well expressed by
Van Loghem, who, along with Van Doesburg, Berlage, Staal,
Romein, Van Vriesland, Wijdeveld and others had founded the Union
of Revolutionary Socialist Intellectuals.

'So there we were in the post-war years, brimful of fine new plans
for the future, to which we had to give shape. They were
wonderful, turbulent years. The shining new cultural era that
beckoned on the horizon, and to which we too were allowed to
devote our strength by carrying the building materials for the
foundations.

The buildings of mankind, the creations in which the liberation of
mankind would be expressed, no longer seemed like visions to us,
but almost as tangible possibilities which would be realized by the
heads and hands of the workers of the new age'. (Lecture, 1928,
quoted in Bouwen, 20/40).

I cannot read such words without some bitterness. On someone
who lives later, and who knows, with the comfort of hindsight, how
the persistent poison of the first world war was to cause the
second, how the revanchist and nationalistic forces were already
preparing the second cataclysm, how everything that was being
dreamed and imagined would be turned into the blackest nightmare,
the train of publications and manifestoes from those first hopeful
post-war years makes an almost unreal impression.

All that thinking, all that work, all those ideas and schools of
thought, were to be shattered like a glass dream. And if you had not
known that some of the ideas of that time had survived through the
muck and mud of 'modern' history and have now, at least some of
the time and for some people, become reality, you would be
reduced to total cynicism.

How venomous can be the frustration of such failed inspiration is
demonstrated by the aftermath of May 1968; on the one hand
absolute materialistic apathy, on the other hand the social suicide of
terrorism. And for the rest: wait and see, and an introverted
individualism, going its own way with its back turned to society.

The idea launched after the second world war by Marshall McLuhan,
that the world is a global village, seems to take shape for the first

ROUWKAPEL HOOFDENTREE (PERSPECTIEF)

ROUWKAPEL PERSPECTIEF EXTERIEUR

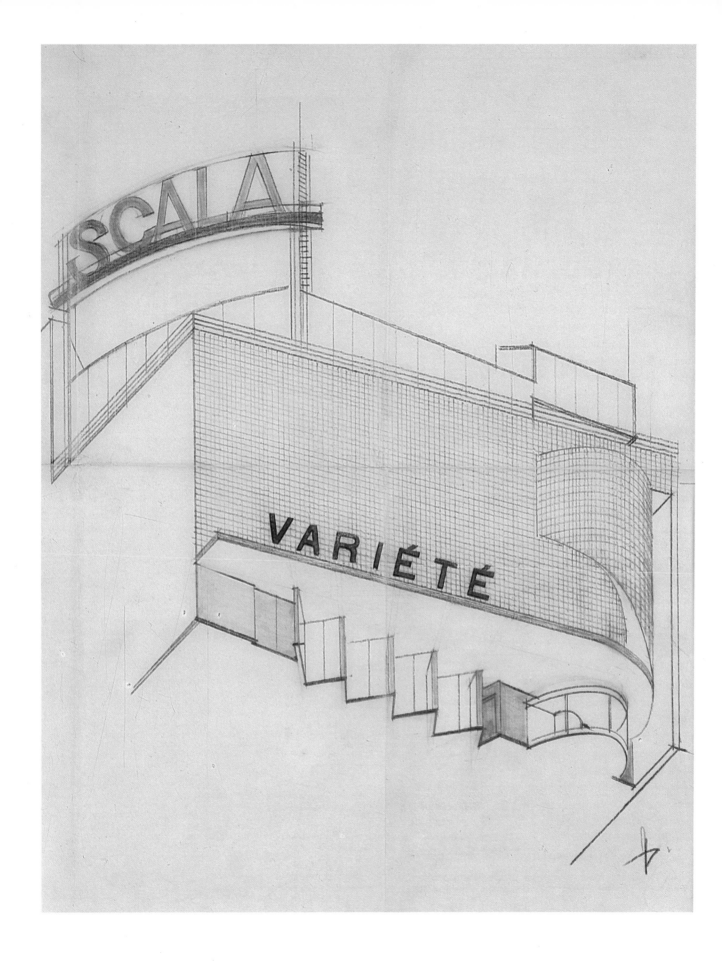

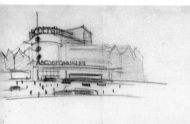

J. Duiker, design for a cinema at
the Kleine Gartmanplantsoen,
Amsterdam, 1930-1934.

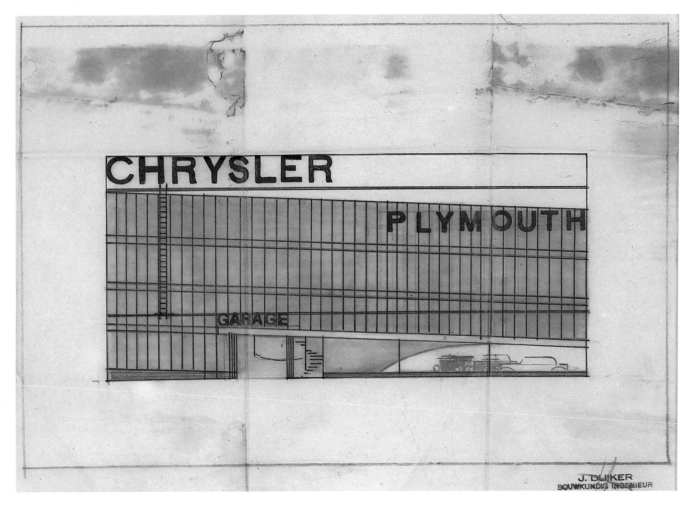

time in the years we are here dealing with. The movement was general, European; people read and influenced one another, saw one another's projects and exhibitions, wrote to one another and went to one another' lectures. Everyone was looking for revolutionary artistic forms for the new social order, which, it was thought, could break out at any moment.

De Stijl in the Netherlands, Constructivism in Hungary and the Soviet Union, Purism in Paris, Expressionism and Utopianism in Germany, Dadaism and Surrealism here, there and everywhere. It is plain that De Stijl, which would eventually have great influence internationally, needed to distance itself from the individualistic ideals of the Amsterdam School. Even the first manifesto of 1918 hits out: '1. There is an old awareness of time and a new. The old looks towards the individual. The new looks towards the universal.

2. The war destroys the old world and what it contains: individual domination in every field.

3. The artists of today, driven by one single awareness all over the world, have participated spiritually in the world struggle against the domination of individualism, against arbitrariness. They therefore sympathize with all those who, whether spiritually or materially, fight for the formation of an international union of Life, Art and Culture.' And by way of further explanation, Van Doesburg added for good measure that their journal wished to 'counteract the archaic confusion – the 'modern' baroque – with the logical principles of a maturing style, based on a pure relationship between the spirit of the time and the means of expression.'

If you close your eyes when thinking of De Stijl, you may, perhaps

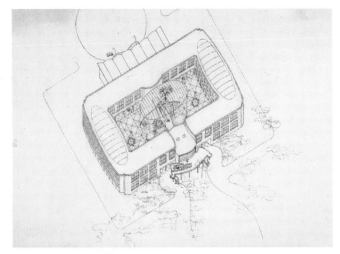

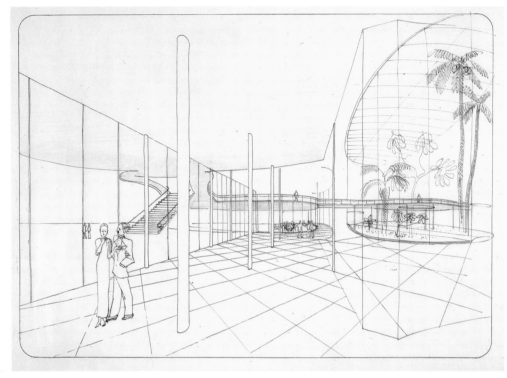

Bodon, Groenewegen and Van
Woerden, idea for an art gallery
with promenade in Amsterdam,
circa 1935.

somewhat unjustly, recall first of all the geometric colour compositions of Mondriaan who' with his primary colours, his completely new organization of two-dimensional space, inspired by French cubism, had become the great forerunner of neo-plasticism. In the first issue of 'De Stijl' he writes: 'Whilst balanced proportion expresses itself in nature by position, dimension and the value of natural form and colour, it expresses itself 'abstractly' by means of position, dimension and the value of straight line and rectangular colour area. In nature we can observe that all proportion is dominated by one primal proportion: that of the extreme one and the extreme other. The abstract representation of proportion expresses this primal proportion of *defined-ness* by a duality of position, set at right-angles to each other.'

In this way Mondriaan seeks a 'perfect harmony' and believes that by

using the rectangle and non-individual primary colours he can achieve a 'universal, cosmic art'. The echoes of his experimental paintings, which struck most of his contemporaries with bewilderment, have so profoundly pervaded our daily lives that the descendants of the bewildered generation do not even notice them any more because they now belong to the 'nature' of the environment.

It is a luxury to listen, while seated on the balcony of the future of that time, to all those voices from the past of *our* time. Voices of actors who have for the most part vanished but whose incantatory, lecturing, ironic, contradicting, persuasive tone has remained, 'There is no material that so rises above matter as does glass. Glass is a completely new, pure material in which most matter has been melted down or converted. Of all the materials we have, glass

G.Th. Rietveld, design for 'nuclear dwellings', 1940.

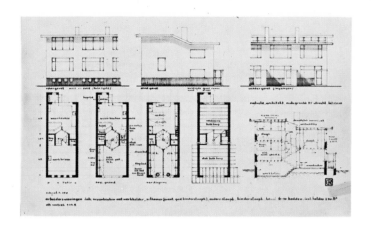

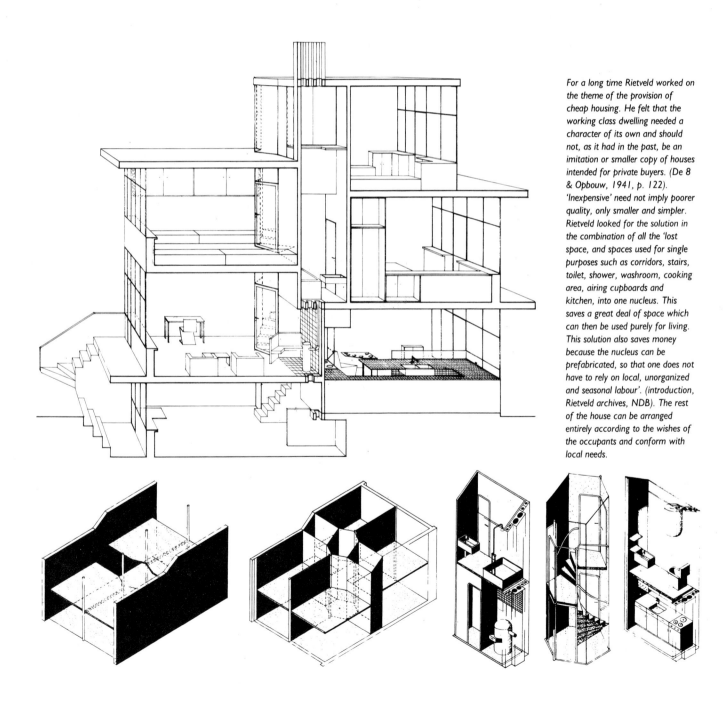

For a long time Rietveld worked on the theme of the provision of cheap housing. He felt that the working class dwelling needed a character of its own and should not, as it had in the past, be an imitation or smaller copy of houses intended for private buyers. (De 8 & Opbouw, 1941, p. 122). 'Inexpensive' need not imply poorer quality, only smaller and simpler. Rietveld looked for the solution in the combination of all the 'lost space, and spaces used for single purposes such as corridors, stairs, toilet, shower, washroom, cooking area, airing cupboards and kitchen, into one nucleus. This saves a great deal of space which can then be used purely for living. This solution also saves money because the nucleus can be prefabricated, so that one does not have to rely on local, unorganized and seasonal labour'. (introduction, Rietveld archives, NDB). The rest of the house can be arranged entirely according to the wishes of the occupants and conform with local needs.

works in the most elementary way. It reflects the sky and the sun, it is like light water, and it has a wealth of possibilities, in colour, form, character, which are truly inexhaustible and which can leave no one unmoved...' (Adolf Behne, *Wiederkehr der Kunst*, Leipzig 1920).
'What is architecture? It is the crystal expression of man's thoughts, of his character, his humanity, his faith, his religion! Once this was so! But who among the living in our accursed times can still understand its all-embracing, bliss-giving essence? Here we are, walking around our towns and cities, and we do not even wail for shame at the deserts of ugliness that surround us...! (Walter Gropius, *Flugblatt zur Ausstellung für unbekannte Architecten*).
'In the distance shines our dawn. Cheers, three cheers for our realm withou violence! Cheers for the transparent, the clear! Cheers for purity! Cheers for crystal! and cheers and ever more cheers for the flowing, graceful, lacy, sparkling, brilliant, light – cheers for eternal building! (Bruno Taut, *Nieder den Seriösismus*, from *Frühlicht*, 1920).

To us, listening to this great chorus of voices, it may seem as if the earth was really empty, as if it would be decided once and for all: culture or nature, individualistic building or mass building,

J.H. van den Broek, competition design for 'Cheap Workers' Home', motto 'Optimum', 1934.

This competition had a good response from architects (92 entries) and the studies of the provision of inexpensive housing that were made prior to it made their influence felt long after the second world war.
Van den Broek sought a solution in open strip-building of four to

twelve residential layers, placed on a north-south axis so as ensure maximum sunshine; only low rise buildings of one and two floors are placed along the north side of the strips, and these will cast no unwanted shadows on the dewllings. The four-storey blocks share a central staircase, while the twelve-storey blocks have lifts and galleries. In the apartments themselves, the children's bedrooms and the kitchen and toilet face east; on the west side there are two living rooms en suite, one of which can at night be turned into the parents' bedroom by means of folding beds. The jury considers that Van den Broek has succeeded in designing 'a type of dwelling that offers many possibilities for living'. (idem, p. 109).

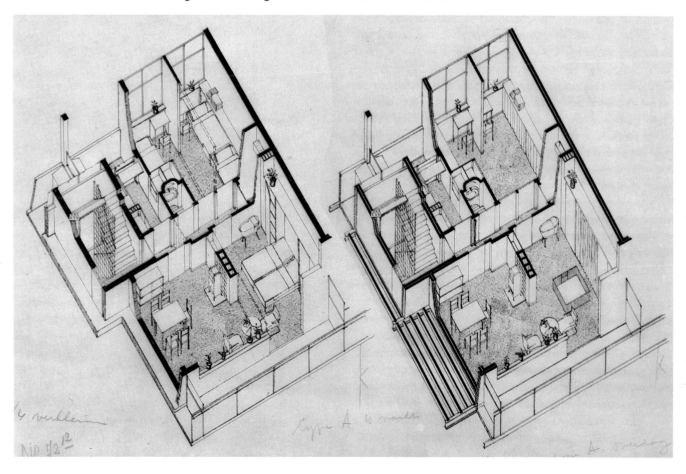

expressionism or functionalism, high-rise or low-rise. Lissitsky recommends the destruction of the traditional: 'the material production must be paralysed throughout the country' – then will begin the reconstruction, 'first in industry and production.' (*Ideologische Überbau*, 1929).

What has, in retrospect, been the influence of De Stijl in those turbulent years? Van Doesburg had few doubts about it. As early as 1927, in the jubilee number of De Stijl, he pointed out that his movement had, albeit indirectly, demolished the romantic post-war mentality expressed by the Bauhaus – and that Le Corbusier had not only seen the Stijl exhibition in Paris but studied it day after day.

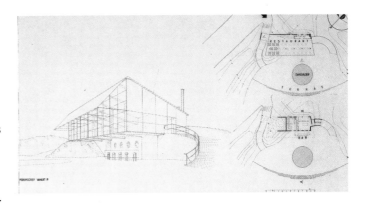

J.P. Kloos, design for a swimming pool in the dunes, Zandvoort, 1935.

The links of the chain join one another not always in too friendly a manner, for while De Stijl's rigorous laboratory research into form and space influenced Gropius and Mies van der Rohe, these two in their turn prepared the rise of the New Functionalism by means of all kinds of technological developments such as skeleton building. The tone is much more prosaic here. 'The New Functionalism starts from the premise – and this might be called its creed – that higher values arise all by themselves if the problems are presented clearly, and are treated and solved in accordance with their nature. From this it follows that these values will be purer in character the more they arise from the essence of things and the less they are imposed from above. Especially this latter point is regarded by the New Functionalists as one of the most important causes of the estrangement that has gradually developed between life in thought and life in action. The New Functionalism tries to bridge this distance, which occurs also in architecture... by consistently taking the view that architecture is a consumer art, which must satisfy ordinary human desires. To do so aesthetically is its ambitious aim.' (Oud, De 8 en Opbouw, 1932).

In the same way as the New Functionalism arose by clearly stating the problem and the position, so it also burst apart. De 8 (founded in 1927 by Merkelbach) did not want a luxury architecture – born from the revelry of line and form of some talented individuals... 'De 8 is a-aesthetic...' so said its manifesto programme – but the breach came because some members could not accept 'the prevailing reactionism in architecture' – and... 'the historical-reactionary' plans of other members.

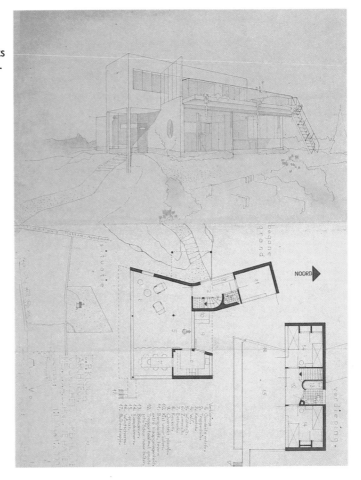

J. Emmen, design for a shore-to-shore link across the New Meuse (Nieuwe Maas) in Rotterdam, 1935.

In 1935, the engineer Emmen designed, by way of counterplan to the recently published design for a tunnel under the Meuse, a cable suspension bridge built so high so as always to allow the river traffic to pass underneath. In order to reach such a height, a long, slowly rising road is required. Because there is no room for this at the chosen site (on the right bank a strip between Parkhaven and St. Jobshaven and on the left bank between Maashaven and Dokhaven), motorized traffic is conducted by way of spirals to the level of the bridge; pedestrians and cycles reach the bridge by means of escalators running right through the spirals. The advantages of this bridge design as against the tunnel design are, according to Emmen, that building a bridge is cheaper and entails fewer risks. The objection that the bridge would obstruct the view of river traffic is, in his view, unfounded because of the tall, slender structure of the suspension bridge.

For the benefit of the Shore Commission which had to choose between tunnel and bridge, Emmen elaborated his plan further in 1936. The only alteration he made was in the ground plan: on the right bank the base of the spiral was moved to the Parkkade, to the right of Parkhaven. Eventually, the Shore Commission decided on a tunnel.

Dutch architecture maintained numerous international contacts. Oud
and Stam co-operated with the Weissenhof Siedlung of the Deutsche
Werkbund in 1927 – where Oud's houses demonstrate most
clearly what the functionalists meant by 'dematerialization'; Berlage,
Rietveld and Stam attended the famous congress of the CIAM
(Congrès Internationaux d'Architecture Moderne) in 1928 in Sarraz,
Van Doesburg lived in Weimar and Berlin and later in Paris, the
journal *ABC*, founded by Stam, published extensive accounts of the
new developments in Russian constructivism, Wijdeveld devoted a
great many numbers of *Wendingen* to Frank Lloyd Wright, and set
up, together with Mendelsohn and Ozenfant, the Académie
Européene Mediterranée in Cavalière.

As a further taste of the spirit and the jargon of that remarkable age
– and to assess the distance that separates us from it – let me
present it once more in its own words: the subject this time is high-
rise building. The conclusion that builders, planners and authorities
were to reach would inevitably influence the lives of the masses.
That it did not always turn out just as they had dreamt, we know
only now – long after the event. Wijdeveld made himself the
champion of the 'tower house'. 'And who shall say whether these
heaven-aspiring tower houses, which now serve only commerce and
money, will not also serve as homes for people in the foreseeable
future? They will not, however, be built because lack of space makes

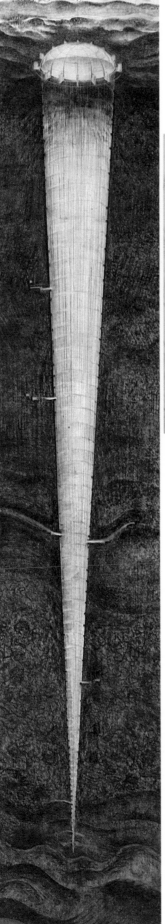

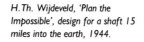

H.Th. Wijdeveld, 'Plan the Impossible', design for a shaft 15 miles into the earth, 1944.

In December 1935, Amsterdam City Council decided to make over the palace on the Dam to the State, for 10 million guilders, and to designate a site at Frederiksplein for the building of a new town hall.

In 1936 a competition was organized for a new town hall at this site. Burgomaster W. de Vlugt described the ideal town hall as follows:

'a Town Hall that will be a grand manifestation of what our twentieth century architecture is able to do, a Town Hall that will in years to come be a testimony to the vigorous life of the Capital City and of its respectful and firm trust in the future'. (B.W.-A. nr. 44, 1936).

The town hall, therefore, was seen as a monument that was to express the power of the city magistrates; there was no mention at all of a town hall being a meeting place for the citizens. What characterized the designs was a very faithful reflection of a time full of political and social uncertainty, reactionary nationalism and fear of the future. Not surprisingly, therefore, the criticisms speak of 'a flight from the present; an anxiety psychosis'. (8 & Opbouw, 1939).

When, after the war, Burgomaster and Aldermen propose to establish the new town hall at Waterlooplein, as part of the renovation plans for the old Jewish quarter, the plans for a town hall at Frederiksplein have become a thing of the past.

their existence necessary, but because of the belief that, through the concentration of technical and economic demands, the most economical solution will be found... The family dwelling is only a cell, an atom within the mass dwellings of the future... But will spiritual peace be found in a dwelling reaching into the clouds, carrying the economy within it, coupling grandeur of thought with broadness of mind, ensuring freedom of action and of life, within the bounds of unity, offering air and light and sun to all, releasing the ground to its fecundity, offering gardens and parks and trees and flowers for the benefit of the whole neighbourhood?... Who is to say whether this is the dwelling of the future?'

Many years after these words were written we know only too well what the outcome of that history has been. Not the final outcome, perhaps, but still... You get an unpleasant, bitter feeling when you see all those manifestoes, ideas, all those movements born from the longing to create a new man by building a new world, against the black shadows of the war, of which all who lived then did indeed suspect the advent, but of which we know that it actually happenend; a war of old people in an old world grown from the spores that had proliferated both above and below ground and that once again proved stronger than all ideals. Now there was no more building in Europe, only destruction. Many of the great plans of those hopeful years lost their last chance of ever being carried out. Not only the built but also the unbuilt was destroyed for ever. It slumbers and dreams on, in drawers and archives, in the show-cases of museums or on the pages of books that commemorate the impossible, until it is brought forth once again — as relic and inspiration, warning and remembrance.

No architect can form a convenient plan unless he ideally places himself in the situation of the person for whom he designs.

J.P. Kloos, design for a Victory Leave Centre at Frederiksplein, Amsterdam, joint assignment, 1945.

After the end of the second world war, Amsterdam became the entertainment centre for Canadians stationed with the occupying army in Germany. Immediately after the war there were few opportunities for amusement in the city. Two Amsterdam citizens, Jules Perel and Maurits Dekker, conceived the idea of building an amusement centre, the Victory Leave Centre, at Frederiksplein.
The centre would have to be designed and built in a short space of time, which prompted the initiators to appeal to the 'De 8' groups of architects. They were asked to submit jointly a draft design for a complex containing: a café-restaurant, various types of bars, a tea-room, a terrace by the water, a variety theatre-cum-cinema, an officers' club, shops,

and a cultural centre. The plan never got beyond the draft-design stage. It probably proved impossible to raise the estimated construction sum of f 200,000, and moreover, the Canadians stayed in Germany considerably less than the fifty years originally envisaged.

An era had come to a close, and it would have become silent in Europe if it had not been for the noise of machines that was heard everywhere. Heinkels, Spitfires, Junkers, the iron rattle of tanks, cannon, anti-aircraft guns, columns of armoured trucks – five years of stamping, throbbing, roaring, shrieking, plodding of machines, which ended only when the last, deadly machine was dropped from a machine on Hiroshima.
Of all the dreams that those machines destroyed, the dream of the faith in the machine was perhaps the most ironic. Again and again, our almost physical infatuation with the machine had come to the fore in the period just ended – the Thing which with its lucid functionalism, would push aside the smudgy individualistic human element. Again and again, this belief recurs, in all manner of forms and comparisons. Oud speaks of... 'the machine, designed to manufacture products that benefit the community more than the artistic products of our time, which reach only the wealthy few'...

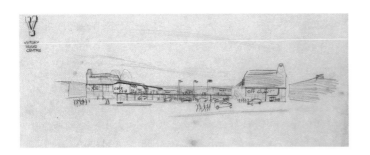

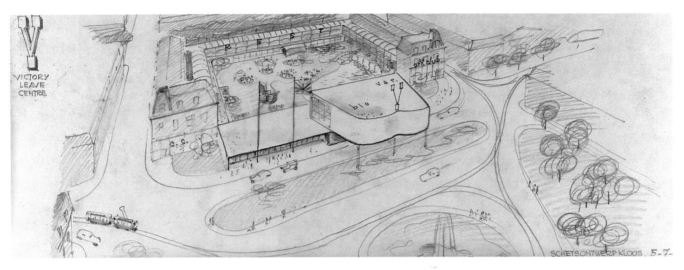

the Italian futurist Sant'Elia, like all futurists, a fierce believer in the dynamic force of the machine, says that...' the futuristic house will have to be a gigantic machine' – the revolution will take place through technology.

The love of machines is not only evident in the domain of architecture. Paul Valery speaks of the spirituality and the mental discipline on which the machine is based, and calls a book 'a machine to be read'. Le Corbusier speaks of houses as 'machines to live in'. To the English critic J.M. Richards a book was 'a machine to think with', the Russian film producer Eisenstein saw the theatre as 'a machine to act in'.

Charles Jencks who quotes these examples in his book *Modern Movements in Architecture* concludes his list with Marcel Duchamp: 'the idea is a machine to make art' and Theo van Doesburg who thought that the machine would be the creator of a new spirituality: 'every machine is the spiritualization of an organism... The machine

is, par excellence, a phenomenon of spiritual discipline... The new spiritual artistic sensibility of the twentieth century has not only felt the beauty of the machine, but has also taken cognizance of its unlimited expressive possibilities with regard to the arts.'

But what exactly is a machine? Harry Mulisch eliminates all such anthropomorphic sentiments from the Thing when, in his book about Eichmann – some forty years and a world war later – he defines the machine as a 'medium without hypnosis'. 'A machine is a rational tool, based on the unquestioned execution of no matter what orders.

A car can do nothing against the 'mystical' command of the foot on the accelerator. It has no possibility of appeal or defence... it has no voice in the matter... it must obey its 'fatum' unconditionally even when the driver is drunk, mad, or dying – because it is a machine.'

It is intriguing to see how two trains of thought meet here. Van Doesburg speaks of the machine as a Platonic being, lofty and pure, free from the muddle and irrationality of 'real' people, whilst Mulisch, on the other hand, speaks of man as a machine: the obeying Thing that Eichmann was.

Of course it is nonsense to say that the machine has done us harm; the atom bomb did not drop the atom bomb; it fell, only after 'we' had let it fall – but on the other hand it can be said that the encounter of man and machine has been fateful – not just in the sense of fatal but also in the sense of fated.

It is strange to reflect that the same Renaissance which, as a result of the 'invention' of perspective, placed man in the centre of the universe, chased him away from there again as a result of the discoveries of Copernicus. It would take rather longer for these to find their application, but once they were soaring through space in

75

the form of satellites, man had changed from King of the earth to gipsy in the universe – preceded by machines.

But there is something else which machines have 'done' for us or soon will do, which, far more directly than was the case with the machine-lovers of the nineteen twenties, has to do with society and therefore with building. The machine has freed us from labour. There is a great deal of unpleasant work, done with, by and around machines, of which the people who used to have to do it were eager to be relieved. Yet now that they have this freedom they do not know what to do with it. Perhaps someone like Wijdeveld foresaw these problems, but society has not yet prepared itself to face them. Society can pay people who do not work, but for the rest it has little to offer.

Hannah Arendt (The Human Condition, Chicago University, 1958) defined the problem sharply: 'Emancipation from labor, in Marx's own terms, is emancipation from necessity, and this would ultimately mean emancipation from consumption as well, that is, from the metabolism with nature which is the very condition of human life. Yet the developments of the last decade, and especially the possibilities opened up through the further development of

J.J.P. Oud, design for the restoration of St. Laurens Church, Rotterdam, 1950.

St. Laurens Church, destroyed during the war, would, in Oud's opinion, be able to serve as a monument commemorating the bombing of Rotterdam. He proposed to consolidate the remains of the church as a ruin, rather than 'restore' a building of which hardly anything remained. However, the city council preferred a reconstruction, which swallowed millions of guilders, and for which modern materials such as concrete were used.

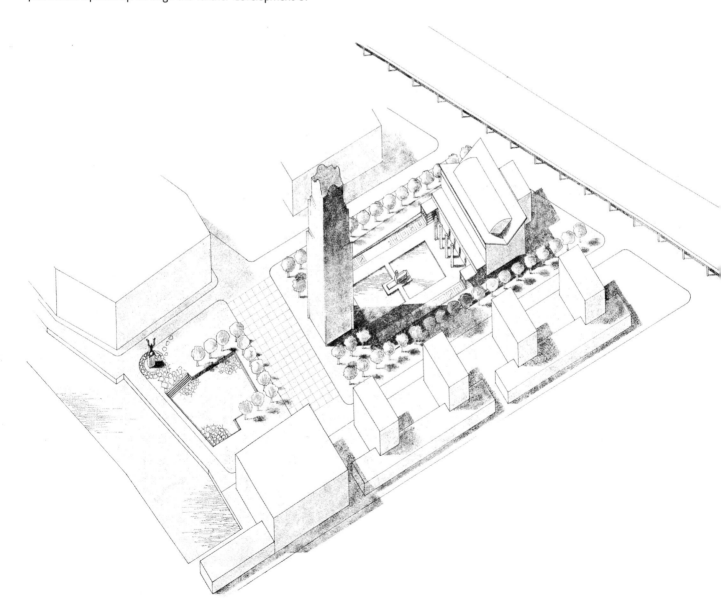

Kloos gave his entry for a second open-air school the motto 'variations on the theme of Duiker/Clio'. After extensive studies, Kloos came to the conclusion that the diamond-shaped groundplan as used by Duiker in his open-air school in Cliostreet in Amsterdam, (1929-1930) is the best. In his explanatory remarks Kloos demonstrates that classrooms whose four walls run from north to south and from east to west receive more shade than classrooms in which the diagonals run north-south and east-west. Moreover, by having intermediate areas (in which there are cloakrooms and toilets) the problems that open-plan classrooms cause each other (noise, mutual visibility) could be avoided. Technical advances enable the appearance to be simpler than in Duiker's school: the floors can be supported by four columns and the walls do not need to carry any weight. This makes it possible to fill completely the south-west and south-east walls with windows that can be opened, whilst the north-west and north-east walls will be blank (protection from wind).

automation, give us reason to wonder whether the utopia of yesterday will not turn into the reality of tomorrow, so that eventually only the effort of consumption will be left of 'the toil and trouble' inherent in the biological cycle to whose motor human life is bound ... with the concomitant serious social problem of leisure, that is, essentially the problem of how to provide enough opportunity for daily exhaustion to keep the capacity for consumption intact.'

And she seems to be giving a direct answer to the vitalists and dynamists of the twentieth century when she says: 'The rhythm of machines would magnify and intensify the natural rhythm of life enormously (rather like the teapot, hurtling down of its own accord, in a famous futuristic painting, N.), but it would not change, only make more deadly, life's chief character with respect to the world, which is to wear down durability.'

What this has to do with architecture is, of course, clear: everything. The magnificent utopias in which these questions were worked out, never became reality. There was never any 'building for future free people', there was only construction for extension of industry, or at best for a host of hedonistic consumers. The masses had to be organized into buildings, the buildings into cities. In his discussion of the role of historical avant-gardes in the context of architecture, Manfredo Tafuri, (*Ontwerp en Utopie*, Socialistiese Uitgeverij, Nijmegen, 1978), reaches the following conclusion: 'Architectural culture between 1920 and 1930... puts all the emphasis on its "political" task.
Architecture – read: the programming and planned organization of building production and of the city as an organ of production – instead of revolution. Le Corbusier formulates this alternative clearly... It adapts the method of design to the idealized structure of the conveyor belt (assembly chain). Forms and methods of industrial labour filtered through into the organization of design... from the standardized element to the cell, the individual building unit, the

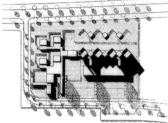

J.P. Kloos, design for a second open-air school, Amsterdam, joint assignment, 1955.

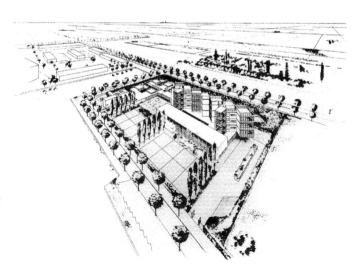

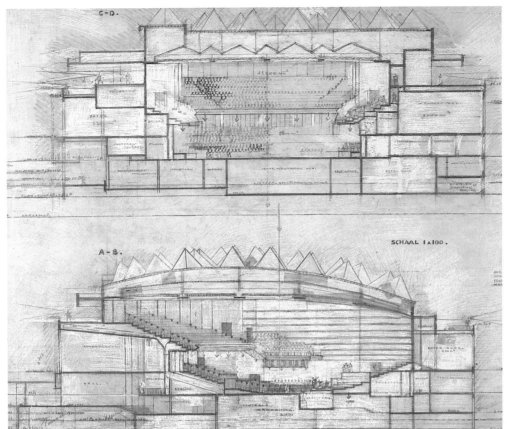

Like all larger cities in the
Netherlands, 's Hertogenbosch
wanted to build a cultural centre in
the nineteen fifties. The city
council therefore issued a multiple
invitation to a number of architects
to submit designs for a cultural
centre in which a music school, a
museum and a concert hall could
be established. The jury, which
included the architects Friedhoff,
Granpré Molière and Oud, was of
the opinion that Klijnen's design
should be selected for further
elaboration. The brief was changed
from cultural centre to congress
and concert hall, the museum and
the music school were dropped
from the programme. Since a
congress building should be
available for use during daytime as
well, Klijnen erected glass
pyramids on the roof to provide
daylight inside the hall. The round
floorplan remained.

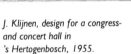

J. Klijnen, design for a congress-
and concert hall in
's Hertogenbosch, 1955.

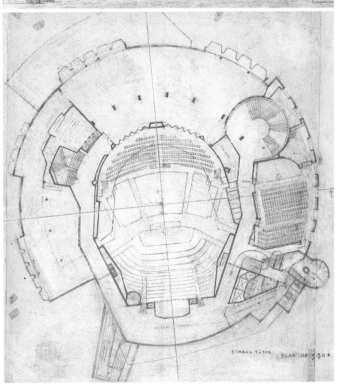

Siedlung, to the city: the architectural culture of the inter-war years
establishes this conveyor belt with remarkable clarity and
coherence...
The consumer is invited to fill the "open" spaces of Mies van der
Rohe or Gropius, and he becomes the central element in the
process... The dream of Morris' romantic socialism — art by all
for all — now takes on an ideal form within the iron laws of the
profit mechanism. Seen from this point of view, the city is also the
last touchstone for theoretical hypotheses.'
The period discussed here by Tafuri could be seen in its totality at
the exhibition Trends of the Twenties. It was Berlin, and 1977, and
there was a tremendous amount to be seen, so much that you
tottered to your hotel each night as if intoxicated, in a state of
spiritual twilight. There were in fact four exhibitions — From
Constructivism to Concrete Art, From Futuristic to Functionalist

W. den Boon, design for a private
dwelling, 't Smalle huis' (narrow
house), 1960.

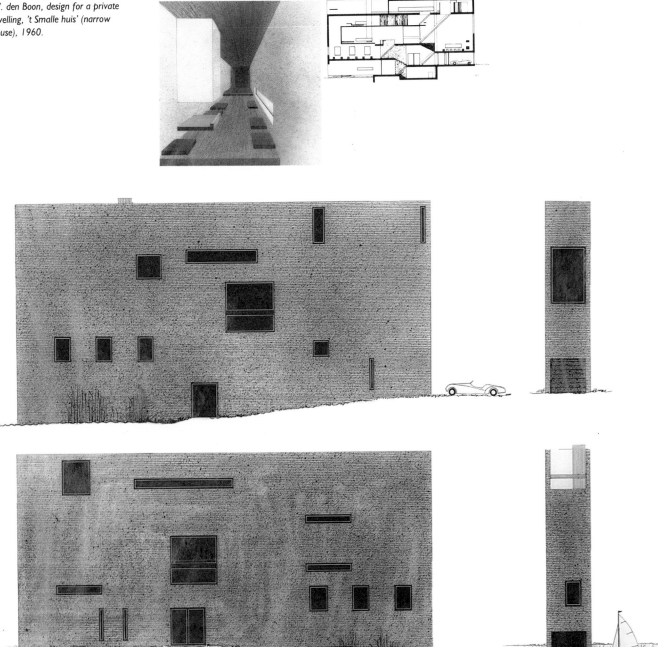

City, Dada in Europe, and New Reality: Surrealism and New
Functionalism; in brief, the whole Big Bang out of which the universe
of modern art — and modern architecture, insofar as present, was
born.

I found it ironic that the exhibition took place precisely in the city
where this whole development had been temporarily but very
drastically halted, in Berlin. This irony of history was noticeable not
only in small things — I saw, for instance, a cartoon by Georg Grosz
of a German soldier being anxiously guarded by two real German
soldiers with carbines —, but also on a big scale, for at the
architectural exhibition all those projects and designs of unbuilt
buildings and cities could be seen in the very city which, through the
actions of a ruler who so much wanted to be an architect, had to a
very large extent been deconstructed.

Moreover, this city, as a result of a decision of quite different rulers,
had now become the showpiece of a very special form of town-
planning. There are not many cities that have a Wall running through
them, and a wall is architecture. So I was confronted with
architecture all day, both at the exhibition and outside. What
happens when you build a wall right through the natural flow of a
city is astonishing. The city suffers a heart attack, in this case a lasting
one. Whenever I became tired of the unbuilt, I went outside and
walked around the unbuilt-upon and along the bricked-up, through
the emptiness and the ruins of an utterly bygone age, to the wall.
Here had been done on purpose what in so many modern cities
happens by accident, through stupidity or blindness: the movement
of the inhabitants, their ability to move naturally to whatever places
they want to go to — Brandenburger Tor, Unter den Linden,
Alexanderplatz; *natural*, self-evident focal points of the city — had
been obstructed, which means that anyone who wants to move

J.H. van den Broek and J.B. Bakema, Pampus Plan, city development plan for Amsterdam, in the eastern part of the IJ, 1964-1965.

City on Pampus was a town-planning study-model of a linear town and at the same time a proposal for a development plan within the IJ lake of Amsterdam, to run in the direction of the IJsselmeer polders, which would thereby become naturally integrated into Randstad Holland. A city for living and working in the IJ for 350 000 people; as many as in Geuzeveld, Slotermeer, Amstelveen and Bijlmermeer together.

Bakema remarks: 'The Pampus plan is a contribution to the solution of the imminent total urbanization of the Netherlands. We believe that present-day concentric developments alone are inadequate and we regard this plan as a plea for a balanced combination of movement and residence without which the concept of a totally urbanized environment cannot be realised…'.

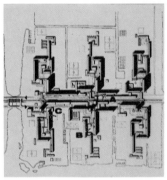

from A to B in this city will, each time he meets the obstacle, also suffer a kind of heart-attack — he cannot go on.

I have tried it out both from the eastern and the western side and it is exactly the same, except that on the western side I found a better observation post: a tall wooden tribune, the ground under which was littered with empty coca cola cans so that you knew exactly who was looking at whom. It was standing by the old Esplanade Hotel, between a wasteland covered with weeds and the boarded-up corpses of the Japanese and Italian Embassies.

On the other side it was empty as well. Watch-towers in which toy people with binoculars stood watching me watching them. Tramrails came to a dead end, men with dogs roamed around the desert as if they were looking for treasure.

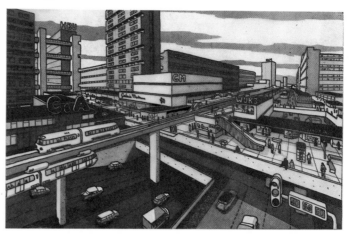

There, by that mysterious, erotic mound, had been Hitler's bunker, beyond it his Reichs Chancery from where he used to go, at night, armed with a flash-light like a thief and accompanied only by Speer, to the Academy of Arts. Two architects of the Unbuilt on their way to look at the plans of their buildings that would never be built. An entire model city had been set up there, mounted on trolleys over a length of thirty metres, in the glare of spotlights replacing the sun. Dutch brick was the inspiration for the soft pink colour of the drawings — but for the rest there was nothing Dutch about it, nor anything human either, because the dimensions of these buildings would dwarf human beings into what it was intended they should be

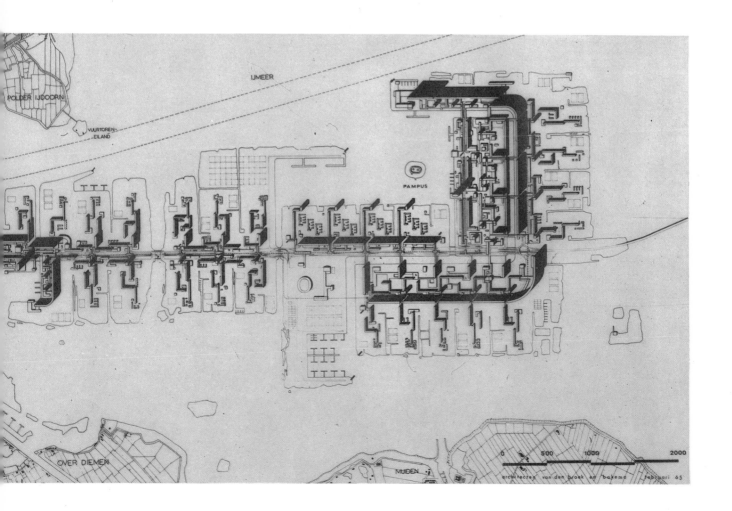

A. van Eyck, The Wheels of Heaven, design for a Dutch Reformed Church in Driebergen, multiple commission, 1963.

To my mind, present-day churches are singularly unsusceptible to ambiguity, in other words, to poetry. I wonder whether it is possible to work with such a negative approach. My answer is: only when you can provide sufficient scope for what is lacking.

Two kinds of centrality? Two ways of being together — or alone? The images are ambivalent — even though the hill reveals what the hollow can conceal: man is both centre-bound and horizon-directed. Both hill and hollow, horizon and centre, are shared by all who sit there in two concentric ways; both bind and both attract (the horizon and the shifting centre, the centre and the shifting horizon). You cannot be together with others

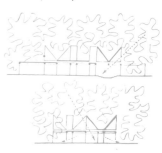

Listening to what this church ought to be and ought not to be, I thought I could detect, among the members of the commissioning body — the Protestant 'Church and World' movement — a certain vagueness, even doubt, concerning the ultimate meaning of a church as a special place.
I mention this because it was precisely this telling uncertainty which gave me the clue I needed.
If I could translate this doubt into a structure, some scope for ambivalent meanings — and therefore also for poetry — might yet result. I was reflecting on twin-phenomena such as inside-outside, open-closed, much-little, alone-together, individual-collective, when the following double image occurred to my mind. And it helped.

in a space if you cannot be alone in it among others.
In order to be able to meditate in a given space, your thoughts must be able to wander — you must even be able to switch yourself off — certainly in a church! The attention need not be drawn exclusively to one central place and to what happens there. No, it should be possible for the attention to roam freely, to a variety of places.
From the outset I wanted the church to be multi-central, but not a-central! I wanted one clearly articulated space (in which the singular encompasses the plural and the plural the singular). The resulting centres or articulated places are not identical to one another, though they are equivalent. There is not even a fixed-place hierarchy; the four-part articulation ensures this. The various centres are closely defined, but their uses are not. I hope they are also multi-suggestive — offering the right scope — for this can be achieved by multi-centrality, (by articulation, not by its absence).

People sitting concentrically in a large hollow in the ground, looking towards the centre, and people sitting concentrically on a hill, looking outward, to the horizon.

Among tall trees: round concrete columns; between these: screen-like walls and, low above columns and walls, a framework of straight and curved beams, a horizontal span, carrying four tall roof-windows in a configuration which, viewed from below, I have called 'The Wheels of Heaven'.

The church opens upward, in several directions at once, thereby incorporating the three tops, but it also opens downward in some places, toward the ground. The area in between is directed inward, churchward, and is translucent rather than transparent.

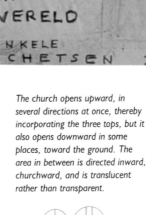

The four circles provide two focal points. These lie on a 'path' running through the entire building, from door to door, and then

further, through two courtyards, into the park. Along this path you 'encounter' two essentially ambivalent places: one for the sacrament of the last Supper? the other for the spoken word?

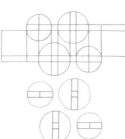

With respect to the complex diagonal pattern: I believe that it contributes to the idea of multi-centrality. The seating arrangement (only a suggestion) makes use of the various implicit directions, so

that different people can experience the same space or the same church service in different ways – depening on where they sit – orthogonally or diagonally, at a distance or nearby. Where the main diagonals intersect, there is, this time, only space!

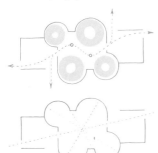

One of the circles forms a small amphitheatre which can be used

for small meetings during the week: christenings, discussions, marriages, music-making or choir practice. The other three suggest circular confines without, however, imposing their centres (all three have been drawn here looking toward the pulpit).

The spaces between the framework of beams and the roof-window construction are, I think, rather mysterious. They are intermediate, a world in between, holding that which is outside and above the roof, and passing it on to those who are inside: sky, passing clouds, trees, birds –

from season to season – and light, which falls through the 'wheelwork' into the space below – and on the people, as it should.

I do not intend to stress the four-part articulation once again by varying the floor-level or by using different floor materials. But the curved balustrades remain. The church is low, only 3.65 metres. If I am lucky, the high fenestration may perhaps compensate for this. I leave that to the wheels.

Aldo van Eyck, 1963.

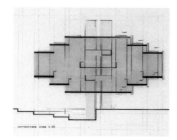 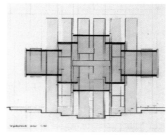

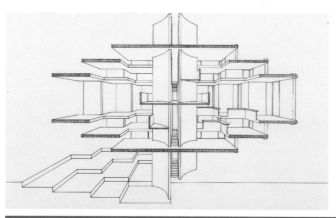

G. Boon, design for a Dutch
Reformed Church in Driebergen,
multiple assignment, 1963.

Altar Garden
An altar like a house
          like a door
          like a roof

          like a hall
an altar like a house
          like a voice
          like a road
          like a bridge
          like a flight of steps
          like a pit
an altar like a house
          like a stage
          like a crossing
          like a porch
          like a belfry
          like an umbrella
an altar like a house
          like a nest
          like a stable
          like a goal
          like a hand
          like a land
an altar like a home
Altar between is altar amidst
an altar on which to play and
          to drink and
          to eat and
          to dance
          at which to sing and
          to listen
an altar to look at and
          to adorn
          to go in and out of
          to sit in and
          to stand in
an altar to lighten and
          to make warm
          in which to keep and
          to air and
          to doubt and
          to reflect
an altar at which to kneel and
          to wash hands and
          to win and
          to lose and
          to film and
          to forget
an altar at which to brood and
          to be sure and
          to make love and
          to laugh and
          to do and not to do
an altar of man
          of animal
          of plant
          of weather
an altar of everything most of all
an altar for conflict
          for coat and dog
          for greetings
an altar for the mist
          for the snow
          for the light
an altar for the fire
          for the wind
an altar for the child

(G. Boon)

84

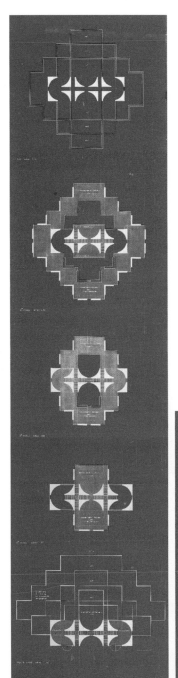

in reality: manipulated dwarves, having to walk under a structure 220 metres high before entering the Congress Hall in their hundred and eighty thousands.

In my thoughts, somewhat confused after so many days of futuristic plans and utopian projects, of festive cities under glass domes, of freedom buildings and machine-love, mass towers and people's theatres, the good and the bad now mingle, and all that remains is the reality I see before me: a wall through a city, and in the dull-glistening light of a German afternoon, the ruins and the new high-rise in East and West seemingly reflecting themselves in each other and refusing an identity of their own.

In the Netherlands of the post-war years, people had other preoccupations. The voices of the ideological debate had fallen silent, the last echoes of the utopias had died away, there were many empty spaces in the country, gaps that needed to be filled. In the language of robust people this simply meant: getting on with it: utilitarian, factory-made building, *a roof overhead*, gasping mass-produced blocks, totally lacking in style.

The holes had to be filled and the regrets would come later. Regrets about the missed opportunities, about quantity at the expense of quality, about unimaginative in-filling. The opportunity of building

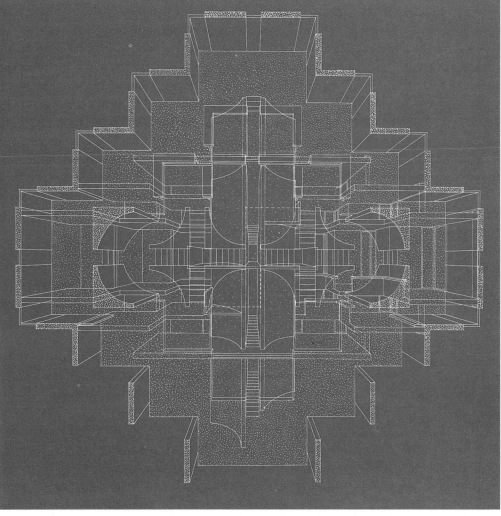

Constant, New Babylon, 1954-1974.

completely new cities arises in few countries, but here, that which every architect of the twentieth century has dreamed of, existed as a real possibility, in the new polders. Almere and Lelystad still had to be built, but alas, the burning spirit did not move those who were given the privilege of carrying out the task. In Almere, childish imitations, a regressive return to an Amsterdam that had never existed; and in Lelystad an empty accumulation of houses which then, by the heart attack method, was bisected by a dual carriage-way as if by a wall. At such critical moments people become the victims of peace-criminals; with the best intentions but with a lamentable lack of vision and spark, a 'living-place' is dredged from the sea-bed.

New Babylon is an entirely new urban environment, shown in maquettes, maps and drawings, in which a world-encompassing, totally industrialized and socialized society could become reality. A city for man at play. The Homo Ludens! The New-Babylonian. In December 1956, Constant visited the Piedmontese town of Alba, where for many years gipsies had during their wanderings been in the habit of setting up camp in the covered cattle market. They lit fires there and hung tent cloth from the rafters for shelters or privacy, and used crates and planks left behind in the market to arrange their improvised homes. The traces left by their presence and the need to have the market thoroughly cleaned by the council after their departure, led the City authorities of Alba to forbid the Zingari to camp on these premises.
Thereafter, they had to be content, during their stay in Alba, with the Tanaro, a strip of grassland along the bank of the river that flows through the town as miserable as any that can be imagined. It was muddy, bleak and comfortless. With planks and jerrycans, the space between a few caravans was screened off: a gipsy-township. After his visit, Constant designed a permanent gipsy camp for Alba, which would form the first stage towards a series of maquettes for

New Babylon, where, by means of movable elements under a roof, a collective dwelling was built; temporary, but always rebuilt afresh and always different; a nomadic camp on a global scale!

Constant says of New Babylon: 'Town-planning is the expression and the image of the social structure of a society, and one cannot make any real changes in it without first changing the society. My designs for New Babylon are not simply architectural constructions; they are basic models for a greater freedom, for a greater flexibility of many different environments that are constantly being rebuilt and pulled down. The true designers of New Babylon, however, will be the New Babylonians themselves.'

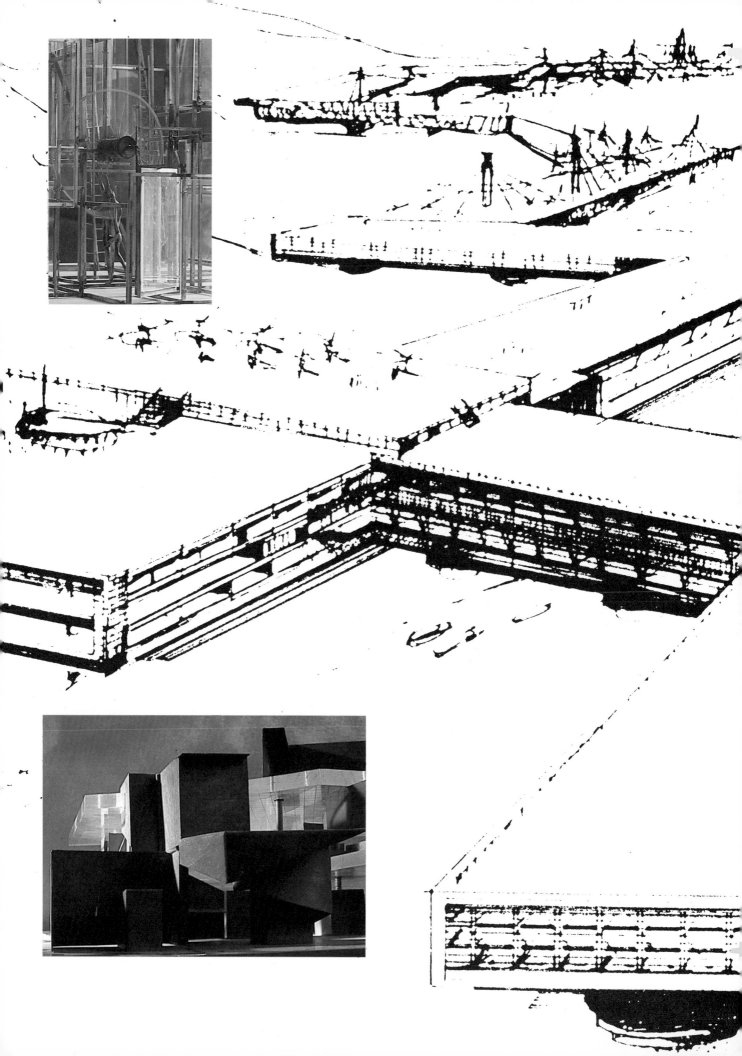

H.Th. Wijdeveld

Only that which is dying, moves, only history is the perpetuum mobile, what is, shifts, even during its birth, as if imperceptibly, into history. The 'now' is a fiction. Only the past and the future live.

Amsterdam has a long history of attempts to acquire a new town hall, after the old one — which had served as a palace for King Louis Napoleon — had passed into the possession of the State of the Netherlands.

Eventually, in 1935, the claim which Amsterdam still had to its old town hall was finally transferred to the State, and in 1936 a national competition was organized for a town hall at the Frederiksplein.

During the war, the design by architects Berghoef and Vegter was designated as the definitive project. In 1945, as a consequence of wartime events, the Waterlooplein became a potential site, and in 1954 this square was designated in principle as the site for the new town hall. The two architects who had won the competition in 1936 were invited to submit a new design.

In 1964 the City Council decided to terminate this collaboration and an international competition was organized. Out of more than 800 entries, the design by W. Holzbauer from Vienna was chosen.

Despite all denials that the Council meeting rooms, which rise above the main body of the building, have a symbolic significance, this became a fierce point of controversy after 1969, and in addition the old argument that 'we already have a town hall at the Dam anyway' was revived once again. This design was the first to experience the full impact of architectural democratization and is, therefore, a symbol of a building designed in 'calmer' times, to be built in a time of transition to the post-1968 design-climate. In the event, this town hall was not to be built after all, because in 1979 the City Council decided to combine an opera house and a town hall at the Waterlooplein.

769

W. Holzbauer, competition design for a town hall at Waterlooplein, Amsterdam, 1967.

A reaction to this wasteland-building came from people like Herzberger, Piet Blom, Theo Bosch, Aldo van Eyck; they put the emphasis on the small scale; the human dimension, and — literally — on individuality. Their publications reveal a profound belief in the creativity of man. Herzberger would most like to build shells with which the inhabitants themselves could then experiment further. The philosophy is turned inward and no longer encompasses the whole world, not even the whole city — no more dream towns are designed, the architect's thinking always remains close to the people, lingers on their door-steps, wanders through their houses, ponders over the relationship between indoors and outdoors, turns away from the big, manipulated ugliness. Titles, programmes, statements are revealing; they can be found in old numbers of Forum, especially in 1959.

'Threshold and Encounter: the form of the space between', is the title of one of the articles, which reflects on the deployment, activations and humanization of the home, and the meeting between earth and heaven. It seems that man wishes to retreat from the wicked outside world, a certain humanizing gentleness betrays itself

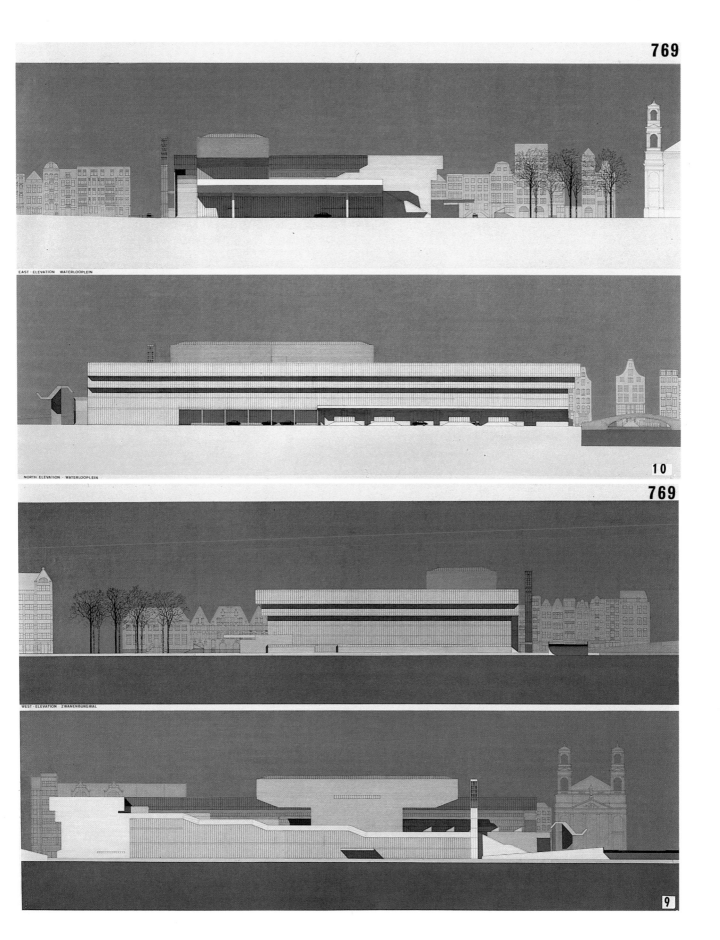

EAST · ELEVATION · WATERLOOPLEIN

NORTH · ELEVATION · WATERLOOPLEIN

WEST · ELEVATION · ZWANENBURGWAL

769

10

769

9

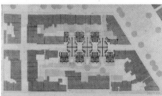

Theo Bosch, design for residential
development in the Jordaan
district, Amsterdam, 1972.

In a redevelopment plan for the
Jordaan, the City Council of
Amsterdam decided in favour of
maintaining the old character of
this neighbourhood. This intention
implied the rehabilitation of the
area and in such a process there
would be scope for many different
kinds of architectural ideas.
Theo Bosch designed a plan for
homes and shops in which the
problem of quality building for low
income groups has been solved.
With this design, the architect
takes a conscious stand against the
'zero-line mania' in which the
cheapest solution is considered the
best.

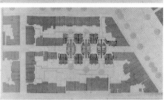

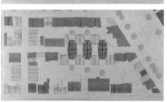

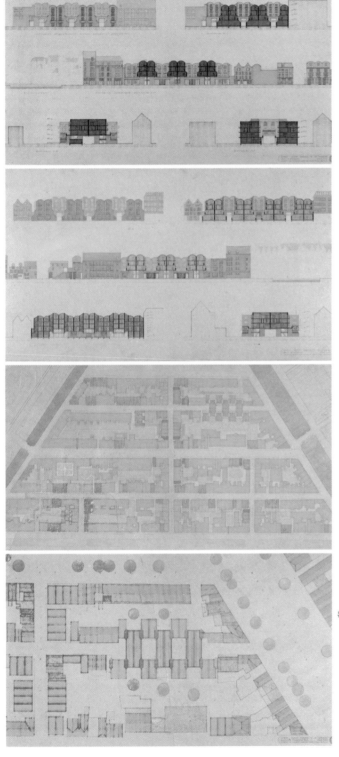

in all these texts, expressing itself hesitantly, not in complete, neatly
constructed sentences, but poetically, in loosely assembled words
and phrases:
house
sphere of the private – personal
enclosed – protected;
I – we in our individuality – inside.
outside
outdoors – the other – the others – fellow human beings –
children …
'One is in the first place human because one is with other people.'
Feeling is here opposed to reason; the wish is felt to turn away from
'coercive form' and 'cold order' and 'chilly perfection'.
'The architect must believe in man' and man 'always remains himself
in spite of all historical metamorphoses'. I doubt whether this is true,
but there is clearly an attempt here to discover an architecture of
warmth, which in the hands of lesser gods, less talented architects,
can easily degenerate into the building of cosy little homes for dear
people, far from the gigantic termite structures of the wicked
world' (*Forum*, September 1959).

However, the dialogue has been resumed. Like a distant relative of
Wijdeveld, Constant appears with his grand concept of New
Babylon. He refuses to accept the culture of today and situates his
dynamic labyrinth in a time that still lies beyond the horizon, a post-
revolutionary culture that has yet to be invented. The gigantic
futuristic problems echoing through Hannah Arendt's writings may

'The Rozengracht in Amsterdam has, since it became a main thoroughfare, always eroded the Jordaan. Perhaps the city as a whole was well served by this heavily used arterial road, but the way in which the intervention was carried out and used has left its effects on the Jordaan.
Part of this small-scale city quarter, this town in its own right, has been amputated.' (Ruud Brouwers, Wonen TA/BK 1972-10).
The Jordaan was divided into a

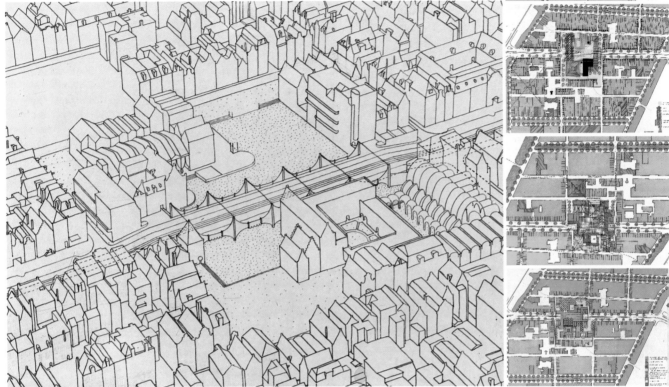

find their answer here. Constant has no fear of automation, certainly not or especially not when it brings with it the complete leisure time society. Man will be able to become a wanderer once again, but this time without being dependent on nature. In the dynamic collectivity of his nomadic people, the combination of all creative forces would bring about an inexhaustible source of inspiration from which every individual could benefit.

Other names, other voices join in the discussion which, since Provo, since May 1968, since 'participation' and 'democratization', has begun to be a merry cacophony. Architects remain this side of the 'great' utopias and seek the answers in the small-scale. They want to allow the consumer to determine his own architecture, they want, like Blom, to allow people to play, or like Van Herk, to render decay harmless and adorn it, to let ;'the quayside lift its skirts', and, thank God, to open up the city to the water once again.

Abel Cahen wants to find a method of handling information and solving problems in successive phases in such a way that decisions, taken at a particular moment, do not in their turn create new conflicts.
'We hope it will prove possible, by means of insight into the structural cohesion and by a constantly alternating examination of the small and the large, to make the complex manageable, so that

North Jordaan and South Jordaan, the smaller southern part being the most threatened. Piet Blom looked for a solution that would restore the unity of the Jordaan.
Halfway down the Rozengracht, Blom proposes a traffic bridge, providing a close link, with various choices of routes, between North and South Jordaan.

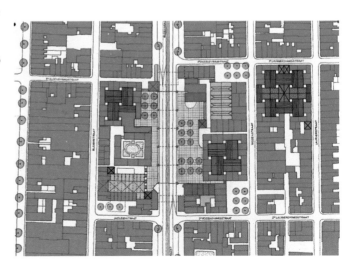

EERSTE VERDIEPING   TWEEDE VERDIEPING   DERDE VERDIEPING   KELDER   BEGANE GROND   TUSSENVERDIEPING

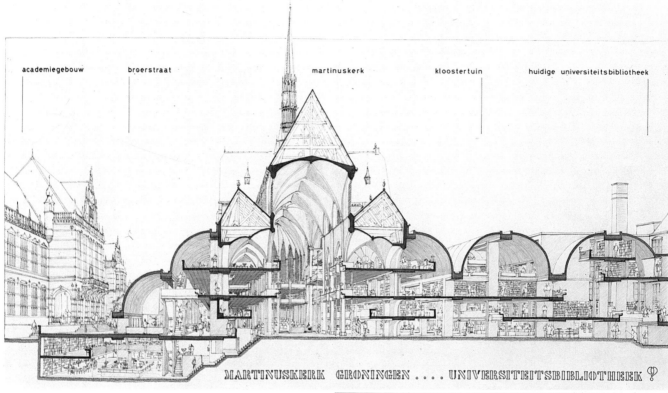

academiegebouw   broerstraat   martinuskerk   kloostertuin   huidige universiteitsbibliotheek

MARTINUSKERK GRONINGEN .... UNIVERSITEITSBIBLIOTHEEK

*H. Hertzberger, design for the
University Library in Groningen,
1975.*

An establishment in the city centre
demands that the university opens
itzelf to the outside world more
than it had previously done, and in
this sense accessibility is the town-
planning equivalent of a less
exclusive, more democratic
mentality. The library should not
only be the memory of the
university but also its
'consciousness', thereby serving as
a gateway to town and
community.
The library must not only make
food available to the hungry, but is
must also stir the appetite of those
indifferent to its offerings. A
library is not only for those already
motivated; it must reach out to the
unmotivated! In that respect the
library should be more like a
modern book store, where you can
enter without having any specific
purpose, and discover, while
browsing, unknown possibilities.
Earlier libraries never suffered
from agoraphobia, as ours do,
which are nothing more than store-
rooms with square metres of
racks: the projection of a utility-
dimension of the mind, hardly

suited to the larger space of the
human consciousness. If
architectural space is the outward
projection of our mental space,
then libraries ought to be given a
different spatial arrangement, one
that is less like memory (which we
possess but which also possesses
us) and much more like our
consciousness and our experience.

92

A. Cahen, Confrontation with a configuration, 1972.

Cahen makes a sketch of an imaginary ideal procedure for solving town-planning problems. Starting off with a set of requirements, an ideal model and a realistic model are designed simultaneously.
In the ideal model, an inventory is made of all the functions to be catered for in the plan, and of their relative densities, and these are then adjusted to each other mathematically.
Each function is visualized in one colour on a grid, by means of balls and circles. The sum of the functions – the ideal solution – is reached by placing the separate grids on top of each other. It will then become clear to what extent certain activities overlap, and one can examine whether these activities are compatible with each other. If they are not, a different solution will have to be found. Cahen calls this theoretical approach the 'abstract design cycle'. 'Working in the abstract and in the concrete phases continues to alternate until all aspects have been included in the programme and in the development of the model, and until all errors have been rectified and all conflicts solved.'
(A. Cahen, Confrontation with a Configuration, in 'Open Research, The Hague, 1972).

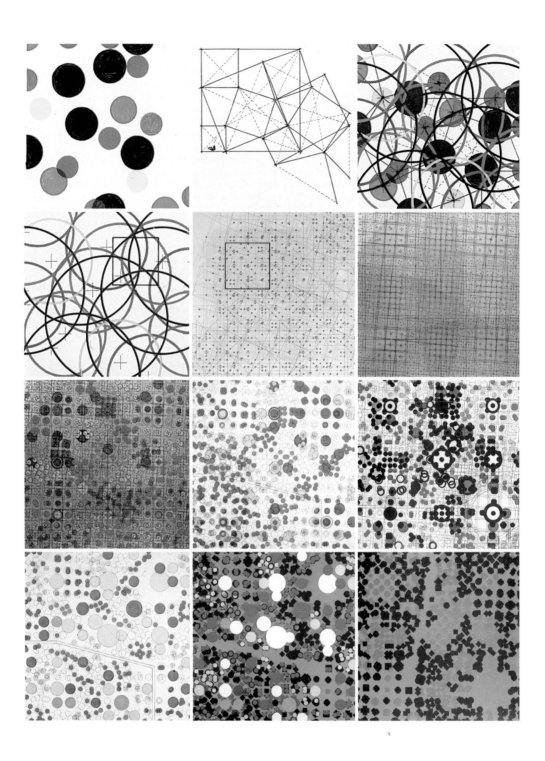

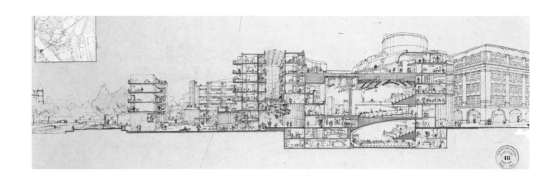

A. van Eyck, H. Hertzberger and others, 'Build something different', Kleine Gartmanplantsoen, Amsterdam, 1976.

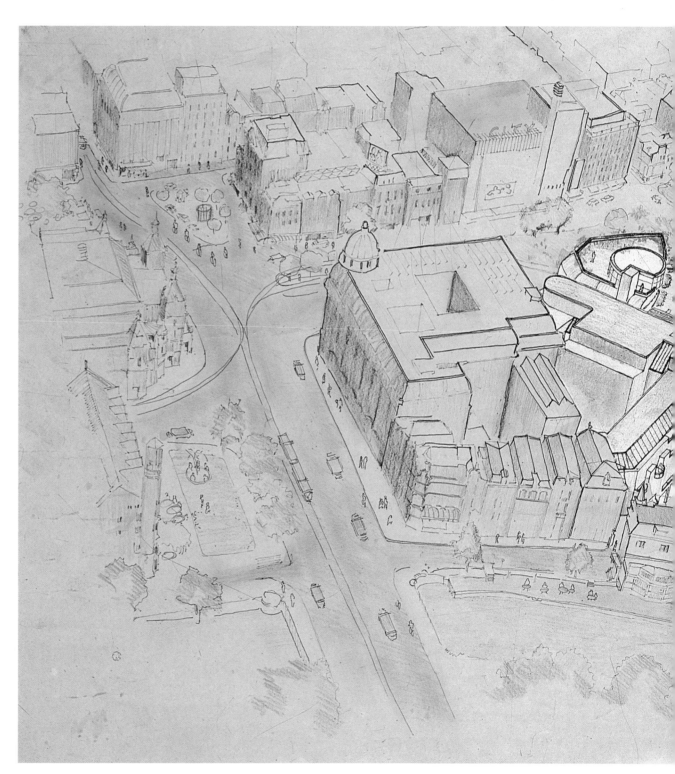

The site of the House of Detention at the Kleine Gartmanplantsoen, which is an area of much speculative building, threatened to become the victim of an overdose of status symbols: luxury hotels, prestigious banks, exclusive shops, prohibitively priced houses and expensive offices. All this, while for a large part of the population no decent homes were to be found.

In 1975 a number of concerned citizens joined together to develop an alternative plan for the whole Leidseplein area, so as to be able, in the debate with the City Council, to take a stand against the plans of project-developer Bouwes. Out of this concern for the city as a whole and for the Leidseplein area in particular, the planning group 'Build-something-different' was born. (The name of the group is a pun on the name Bouwes. Trs).

The starting point of 'Build-something-different' was to try to design a plan based on a totally different mentality. In consultation with the public, architects Dijkstra, Van Eyck, Hertzberger, Van Klingeren, Klunder, Rietveld and Verster worked out a plan in three months.

The jointly drawn-up programme of requirements included a theatre, cinema, an art centre, a creative-and-educative centre, a concert hall (Paradiso), a legal aid office, a centre for foreign workers, a reception centre for young working people and a photographic centre. There would also have to be shops, small offices, catering establishments and dwellings. The solution suggested by the seven architects was not a definitive plan, it was a 'printer's proof', an inspiring plan for discussion, which might result in both the programme of requirements and the plan for the environment being improved and becoming more specific.

full justice may be done to the small and the individual, as well as to the opposite.' (*Wonen*, 3rd year, nr. 8) He is against the 'unacceptable simplification of complexities'; in fact he wants to study the complexity which used to constitute the soul and the life of the old city, so as to be able to recreate it. If this method had been followed in Almere, the town would have looked very different.

Koolhaas, in an interview with Max van Rooy (*NRC Handelsblad* 17-11-'78), rejects the architecture of 'fellow-humanity':... 'even in the technological courses at Delft there is a gruesome striving for hospitality and human warmth. Seen cumulatively, architecture is regarded as psychological therapy. The public is diagnosed as being in need of help and therefore in need of architecture....
The alibi of the human factor leads to a crazy amateurism and architectural gobbledygook, to naivety and to that absurd curse: the duty to communicate. Whatever design I make has to satisfy myself. It has to please *me* and it is the tragedy of the postwar situation that architects are forever creating inhabitants to whom they do not themselves belong. This leads to condescension.'

The circle, our long circumambulation that started at Galman's bridge over the IJ and ends with Benthem's Rijnmond Tower, is complete. The long discussion, the vehement arguments, die down and silence returns to the great city of never-built buildings. I imagine I am alone now, I imagine that for once, very briefly, these buildings

Present state

Anatomy lesson

All dilapidated parts are demolished

Creative restoration

New spirit in old building

White ruin

Accompaniment of the decay

Decay and future

*A. van Herk and C. Nagelkerke,
creative restoration,
Haarlemmerpoort, Amsterdam
1974.*

*Creative restoration
Haarlemmerpoort-Amsterdam.
A dilapidated monumental
building, neglected as a
consequence of fundamental
changes in the city scene. In 1974:
a meeting point for a group of
artists and architects opposed to
the blind imitation of the past in
contemporary building and
restoration. Current methods of
conserving monuments are called
into question and the concept of
creative restoration is put forward
instead.
The plan demonstrates three
phases, after the building has been
freed from its historical ballast.*

*White Ruin
The accent is on the basic shape,
with the intention of glorifying the
monument in its purest
architectural form.*

*Metamorphosis
Rough wooden props, needed to
hold the dilapidated building
together, grow into a second skin
behind which the original form is
concealed and to which additions
are made.*

*Blending of styles
Worn parts are not restored to
their original state but replaced by
contemporary forms and materials.*

*The plan intends to inaugurate the
renewal of a historic building
marked by neglect and decay.*

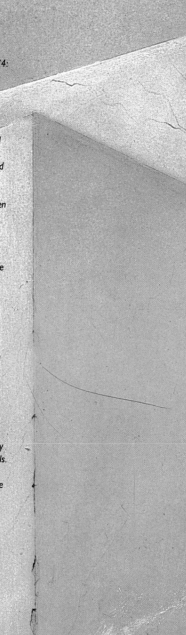

really exist. Here I walk, in the soundless universe of a dream. I stand in the vast empty square by the IJ, I walk past the Pantheon of Mankind, I see in the distance the Byzantine cupolas of Bauer's theatre, stroll past the new, monumental Haarlemmerpoort. What would it have been like? We shall never know, and yet the question imposes itself.

What would it have been like? Would we have become different? Yes. The built, if it had not remained unbuilt, would have seeped into our consciousness like everything else around us. It would have become part of our memory, of our daily lives. It would have featured in a thousand photographs; Vestdijk, in his novels, would have made his characters walk past them, we would have sat in those theatres watching plays by Hugo Claus, we would have demonstrated in front of those buildings, they would have entered us as we would have entered them. Sometimes we would not have seen them because, by always being there, they would have become as invisible as real buildings, like the Palace at the Dam or the Rijksmuseum. They would have changed us simply by being there. Ugly or beautiful, they would have become the backdrop to our lives, and therefore part of us. That is why this book is also a portrait of ourselves. In the not-built we see ourselves as we have not become. A part of us that has never existed closes together with the last page.

C. Weeber, design for a central library in Rotterdam, 1977.

In 1977 the City Council of Rotterdam invited J. Bakema and C. Weeber to submit designs for a central library on a site at the Blaak. The assignment stipulates that the library should be regarded as a place where anyone in search of information is welcome, and the architecture must be an expression of this principle.
Weeber's library building fits in with the existing surroundings

which consist of closed blocks. The walls of his library follow the lines of the adjoining frontages. 'As a building, the library is not conspicuous: it forms part of a block. It can be distinguished and recognized only by the appearance of its facade.' (Wonen, TA/BK 1978, nr. 9, page 10). It can be noted, then, that Weeber has not made his building open outwards, but the interior lay-out is clear and well-ordered.
'In my view, a public building must be very clear, especially inside, so that people who do not go there very often, will immediately know as they enter how the place is arranged and where they can expect to find this or that item'. (idem, p. 9). However, his design was rejected by four out of the five members of the jury, as 'not inviting enough'.

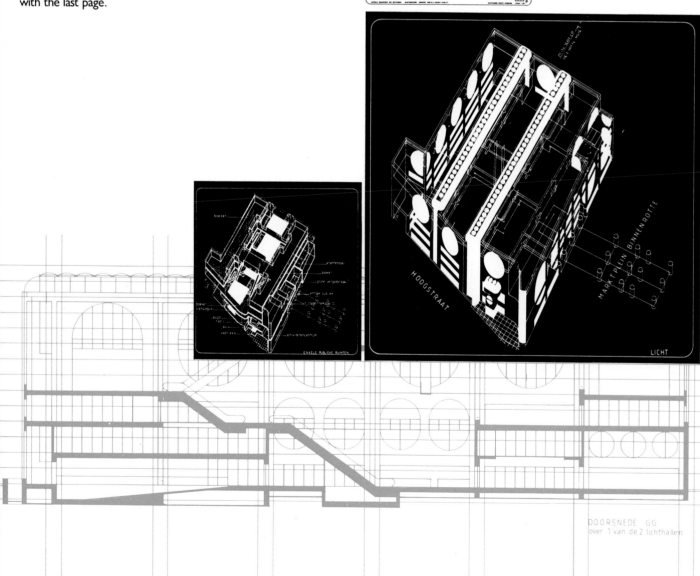

ELEVATION NORD DE LA STADSKAMER PENDRECHT

0 1 2 3 4 5m.

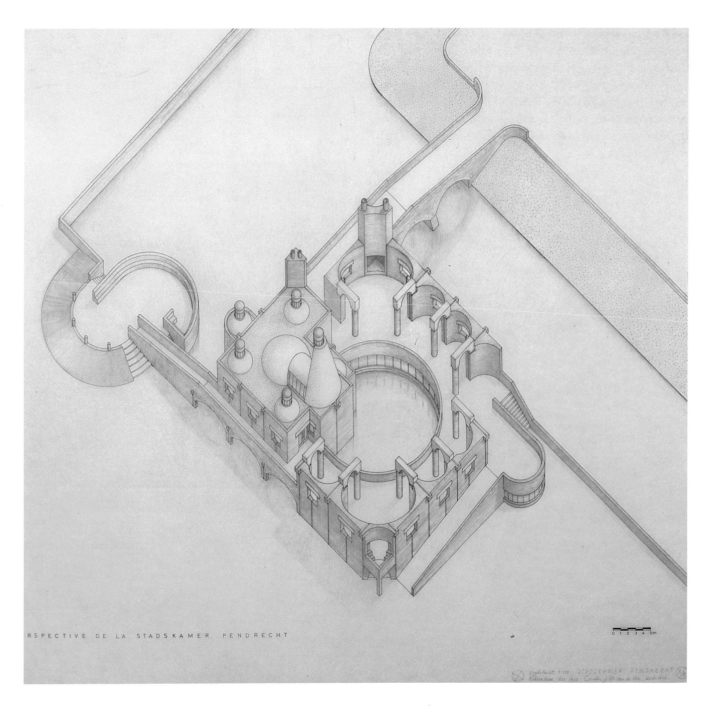

RSPECTIVE DE LA STADSKAMER PENDRECHT

0 1 2 3 4 5m.

98

C.J.M. van de Ven, 'Civic Hall for Pendrecht'.
Design for a community centre at Plein 1953 in Pendrecht, Rotterdam, 1975.

In the summer of 1975, the Rotterdam Arts Foundation took the initiative to ask architect and town-planner Cornelis van de Ven to develop a plan for Plein 1953. The resulting project by Van de Ven, which he called 'Pendrecht Civic Hall', dealt with the problems of Plein 1953 and with the growing need for a community centre.
Van de Ven says of his design: 'The Rotterdam district of Pendrecht is

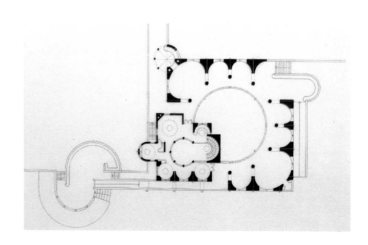

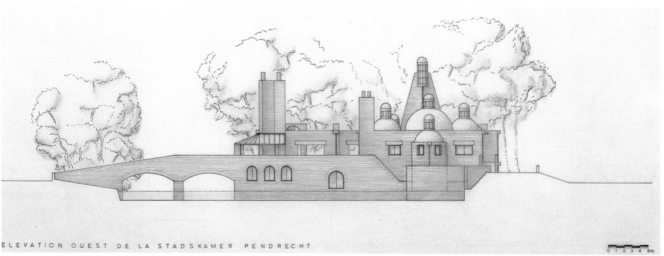

ELEVATION OUEST DE LA STADSKAMER PENDRECHT

built up out of four quarters around one centre of gravity. These quarters are further subdivided into residential neighbourhoods of seventy to eighty dwellings, arranged around a play area. This downward progression in scale from district to quarter to neighbourhood to individual dwelling could have given the inhabitants a sense of identity. In reality, only the neighbourhood has become a recognizable unit. The first grade of scale, that of the district, still seems to be inadequately structured.
The central space, Plein 1953, lies at the geographical and commercial centre of gravity of the district. However, as an emotional focal point for the life of the area, this central square has so far been sadly unsuccessful. There is nothing in the appearance of this important square to suggest its unique quality. Moreover, it is hardly distinguishable from the stereotyped shopping precincts in other development areas.
This phenomenon is closely connected with the New Functionalist ideology: since the CIAM Congress in Frankfurt, quantitative housing requirements have become crystallized into

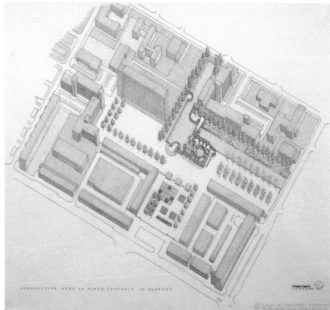

norms that are supposed to guarantee the 'Minimum Existence'. ('Existenz-Minimum'). This ideology of interior space entailed that the outside space between the residential blocks was maximized. The phenomemon of the minimum interior space as opposed to the maximum exterior space can be called the paradox of

New Functionalist town-planning. This is particularly true of Plein 1953. Pendrecht is a composition of exterior spaces; my proposal for 'Pendrecht Civic Hall' intends to offer a necessary addition to this: an urban interior space.' (Plan, 4. 1977, page 32).

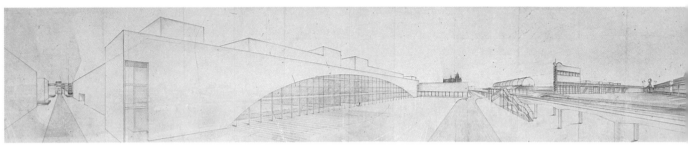

A. van Herk, S. de Kleyn, F. Kurvers, G. Urhahn, design for 'the city on the IJ' in the eastern dock area of Amsterdam, 1979 1980.

Above
Panoramas now and in the future.

Above left:
New town frontage on the IJ, emphasizing the contrast between land and water.

Below left:
Large square for the whole of Amsterdam, with splendid views of the IJ and the city skyline. This square forms the link with the roads leading to the surrounding areas.

Right:
Building on existing strips of land and on constructions in the water with new shore to shore connections across the IJ, between Pampus and the North Sea Canal. Here a pedestrian and cyclists' bridge through Central Station: gateway to the eastern dock area and to Amsterdam North.

The eastern dock area of Amsterdam: abandoned and boycotted by ocean-going ships that once filled the harbours (1977).

Central Station and railway embankment robbed Amsterdam a hundred years ago of its view of the IJ. At the same time, the inner harbours were no longer accessible to ocean-going vessels. The eastern docks area became an outer harbour in the IJ, not integrated in the life of the city, but preserving a characteristic feature: its openness, because of its harbours and land spurs pointing towards the sea. The question is now:
How to use a unique opportunity for Amsterdam to open out towards the IJ once again, by bringing about an interaction between an abondoned harbour and an overcrowded city. The starting-point in this plan is an analytic and imaginative attempt to discover the essence of the new urban space.

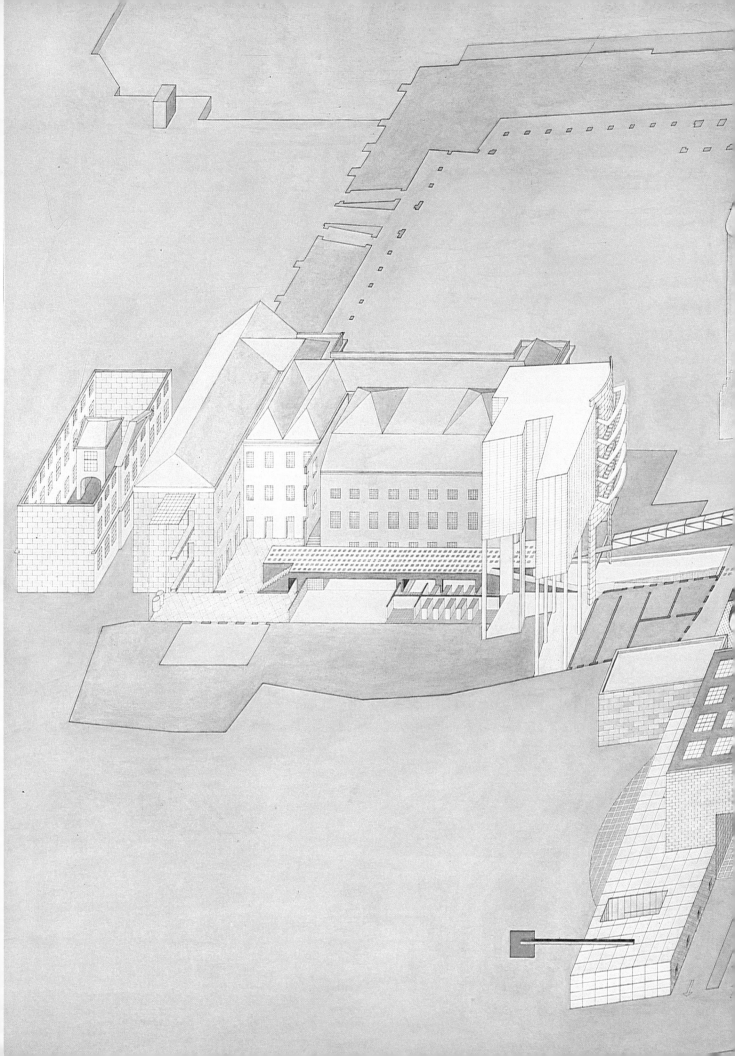

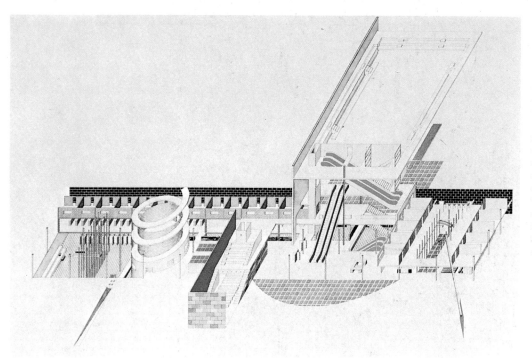

Koolhaas' suggestion to erect a long, narrow building beside the Binnenhof and to link the two by a high-level bridge, met with both opposition and approval. Supporters pleaded for this stimulating project to be carried out.
'... a mutant form of town-planning, new types of architectural scenarios that can result in the rehabilitation of the Metropolitan life style – that accepts the Megapolitan situation with enthusiasm and wishes to return to the architecture of the big urban area with its mythical, symbolical, literary, imaginary, critical and popular functions...'

Office for Metropolitan Architecture (O.M.A.), Zaha Hadid, Rem Koolhaas and Elia Zenghelis. Competition design for the extension of the Second Chamber buildings, 1977.

On 13 July 1977 Minister Gruyters of Housing and Environmental Planning organized a competition for the extension and renovation of the Second Chamber.
One hundred and eleven entries were received, but contrary to all expectation, the jury considered none of the designs to be suitable. This had happened before. The competitions of 1863 and 1922 had also led to nothing; in both cases the politicians found the construction costs too high.
This time it was different. The nature of the designs, not the he cost, was the obstacle to building work on the Second Chamber. Although neither money, effort nor materials were spared, no plans were produced to which the jury was able to give its blessing. A host of questions were asked. Was there a lack of quality among Dutch architects? Did the best architects not take part in the competition? Was the jury incompetent? Was the jury competent but misguided? Was a competition the right approach to this kind of problem? Was the brief badly set out? Does a competition have any chance of success in the present climate in the Netherlands?

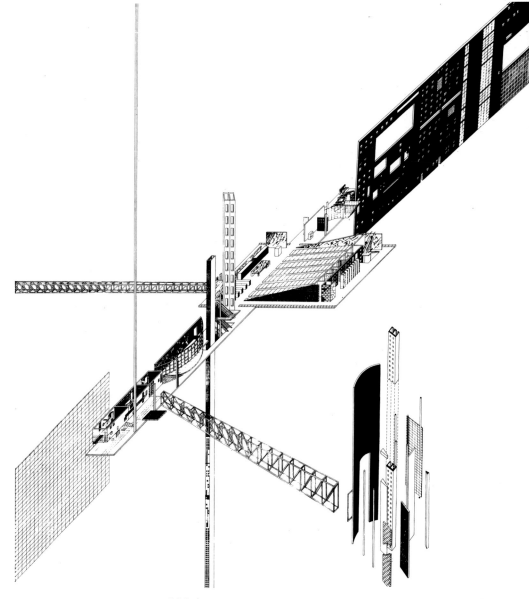

TOMMYGUN TOWER

DILLINGER, dil'in-jer, **John** (1903–1934), American criminal. He represented the new kind of criminal that appeared in the United States, particularly in the Midwest, as the Depression of the 1930's deepened.

Unlike organization mobsters, such as Al Capone, the Dillinger-type criminals did their own shooting. Made mobile by the motorcar, they would rob a bank, then race across a state line to safety. Their daring impudence in those days of disorganized law enforcement led to the strengthening of the Federal Bureau of Investigation. Among them were Baby Face Nelson and Bonnie Parker and Clyde Barrow, but it was Dillinger who most captured public imagination.

He was born in Indianapolis, Ind., on June 22, 1903. After spending nine years in a reformatory and prison for a youthful crime, he emerged, embittered and schooled in crime by professionals, to become in 13 hectic months the most notorious bank robber since the James brothers. He was captured twice, escaped jail twice, and fought his way out of numerous traps. Finally he was shot down on July 22, 1934, outside Chicago's Biograph Theatre by federal agents tipped off by his girl friend's landlady, "the woman in red."

H. Tupker, competition design for a Chicago Tribune Tower, 1980.

The competition for the Chicago Tribune Tower in 1922 was a highlight in the architectural history of the twentieth century because all the major architects of that time (Gropius, Scharoun, Loos, and, from the Netherlands, Duiker and Stam and others) took part in the competition and produced, in some cases, very personal ideas for 'the most beautiful office building in the world'. In 1979, two architects from Chicago, Stanley Tigerman and Stuart Cohen, conceived the idea of repeating this dramatic event and invited a large number of architects from all over the world to design a new office tower block at exactly the same place and with the same programme as in 1922.

In their invitation the organizers state that with the aid of the entries for the competition of 1922, the various trends in present day architecture can be seen in a broader perspective. It is the intention that, with this new competition, 'the period of vitality and change which characterizes architecture today' should be documented.

Tupker's design displays formal similarities to a machine gun, but also with the Statue of Liberty in New York. By way of explaining his design, Tupker gives a brief biography of one of the greatest criminals of America: John Dillinger.

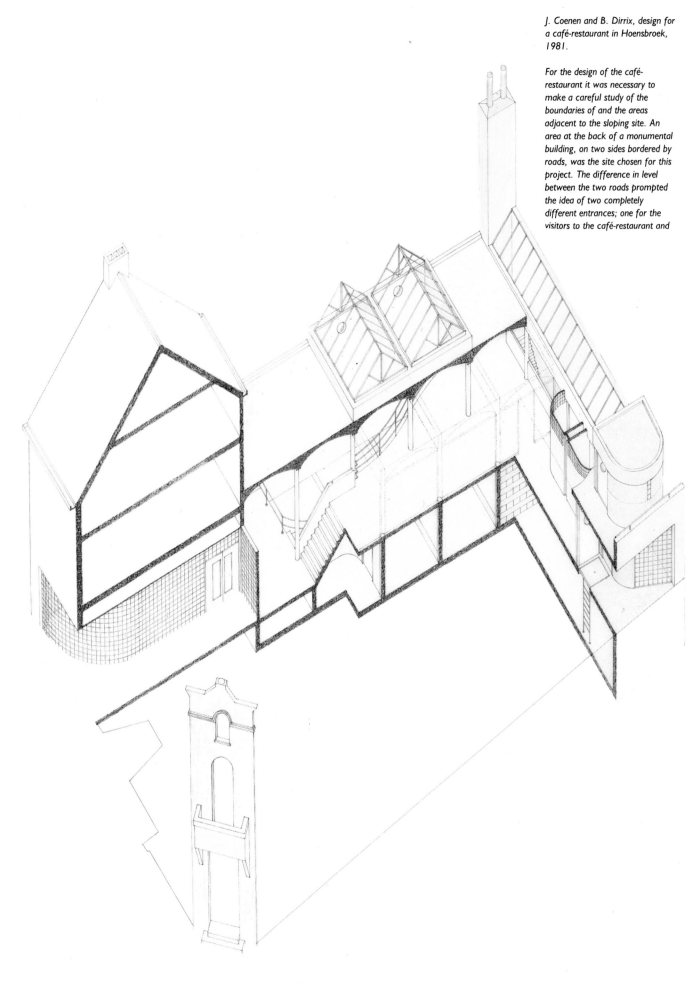

J. Coenen and B. Dirrix, design for a café-restaurant in Hoensbroek, 1981.

For the design of the café-restaurant it was necessary to make a careful study of the boundaries of and the areas adjacent to the sloping site. An area at the back of a monumental building, on two sides bordered by roads, was the site chosen for this project. The difference in level between the two roads prompted the idea of two completely different entrances; one for the visitors to the café-restaurant and

the other for the occupants of the
apartment above as well as for the
provisioning of the kitchen.
The restaurant is in principle a 6
metre high room, roofed over with
barrel vaults and glass, linking the
main street and the side street. The
difference in level between the two
entrances is bridged by a balcony.
At the lower level are the café and
the dining-room with their own
entrance, as well as the kitchen; at
the intermediate level are the
balcony, the toilets and a fire
escape, whilst the highest level, the
roof, gives access to the apartment
and leaves room for a terrace.

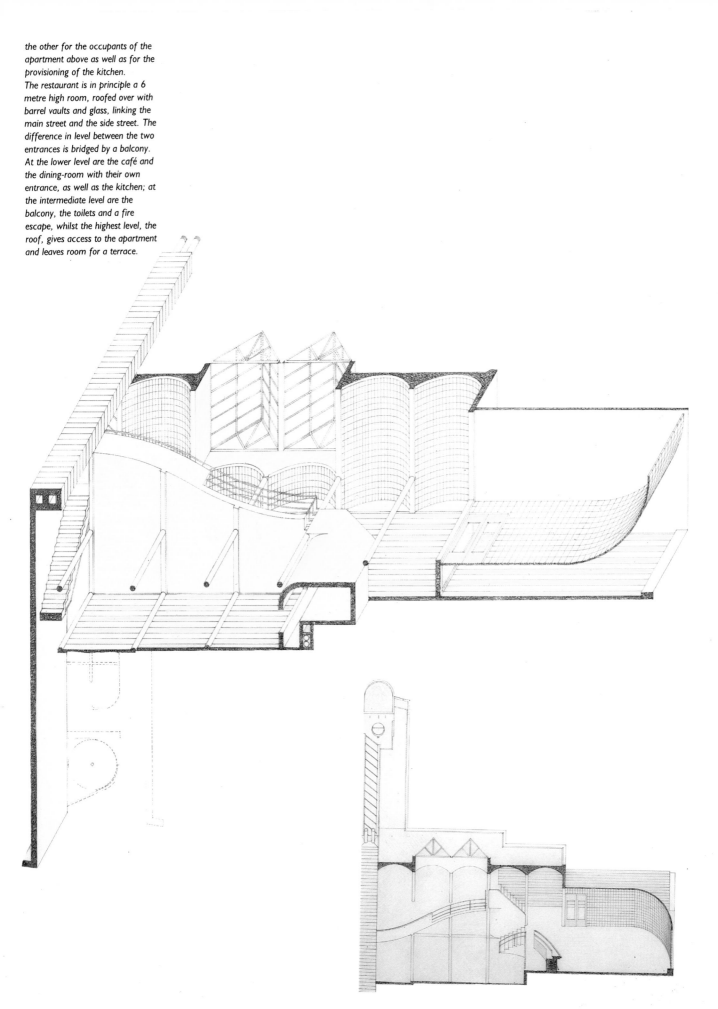

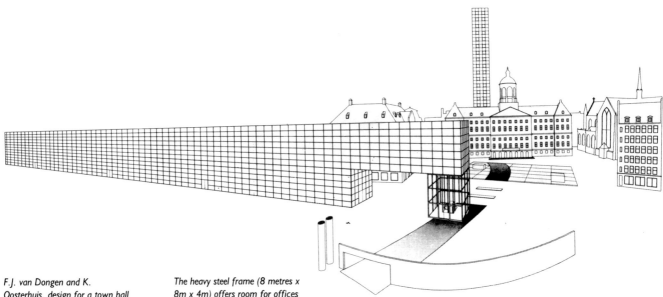

F.J. van Dongen and K.
Oosterhuis, design for a town hall
at the Dam, Amsterdam, 1980.

The centre of Amsterdam is the
only proper place where all the
requirements of a town hall can be
fully met. In this project, the
programme has been divided into a
representative, an administrative
and a 'democrative' section.
Representative.
The Palace at the Dam is to be
transformed into the representative
section. The Civic Hall is to be the
scene for the representation of life:
here there will be rooms for the
registration of births, marriages
and deaths.
A dark, smooth marble executive
tower, in which burgomaster and
aldermen have their offices in
vertical order of rank, rises
towards heaven at a site which
history had unconsciously reserved
for new developments.
The long administrative building
containing secretariat, archives
and, on the ground floor, reception
desks, presents a gleaming facade
to the Rokin side. A row of five
sunken pneumatic caissons lies at
the base of the building. The linear
character of the building can be
seen internally in the almost
endless repetition of the open
metal grid structure, flanked on
both sides by a flared perspective.

The heavy steel frame (8 metres x
8m x 4m) offers room for offices
of whatever dimensions are
required. Alongside, on two sides,
there is a wide air-conditioned zone
and a traffic zone. A mirrorlike
surface expresses the symbolic
nature of the building.
Democrative.
The democratic tournament takes
place under ground. In the meeting
rooms under the Dam the
battlefield extends from the council
chamber at one end (linked to the
executive tower) to the circular
general information centre at the
other. Behind a slightly curved
glass screen there are areas where
the participants in the game can
refresh themselves physically and
spiritually. Above ground, the
information centre looks like a
projection screen. A glass light-
strip follows the course of the
democratic process. An open steel
cube has a dual function: it forms
the entrance to the underground
assembly area and also gives
access to the restaurants in the
projecting part of the long
building.
The autonomy of the
programmatic parts is
strengthened by the fact that
content, appearance and
construction mutually confirm one
another.

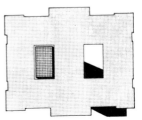

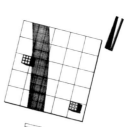

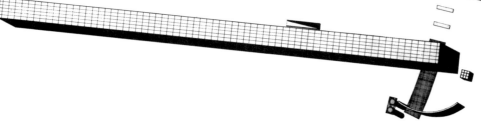

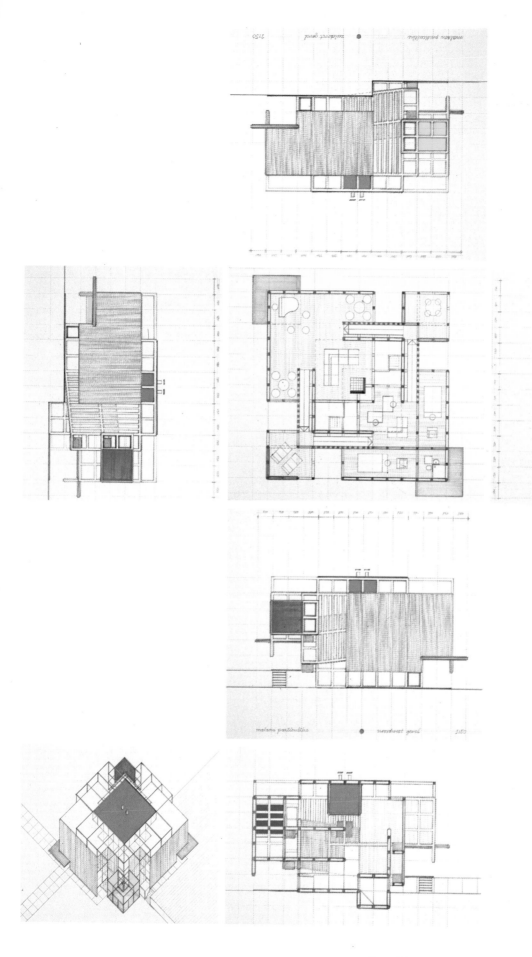

zuidoost gevel   middelen perkelkuben   1:50

maison particulière   ● noordwest gevel   1:50

D. van Woerkom, design for
Maison Particulière, II, 1982.

A preoccupation of De Stijl in the
twenties was space, supported by
colour. As Van Doesburg and Van
Eesteren put it in 1923: 'We have
examined the laws of space and
their infinite variations (that is to
say, the contrasts between spaces,
the dissonances of spaces, the
complements of spaces, etc.) and
we have found that all these
variations can be controlled in a
balanced whole)'. Nevertheless, the
results of this examination are such
– in respect of 'continuing space',
the spatial ideas of Van Eesteren
and Van Doesburg were fairly
conventional – that after 1955
this study was continued in the
journal 'Structure', with the adage:
'In synthesist architecture,
architectural space is seen to
consist of a number of functional
spaces, continuously opening into
each other, thereby at the same
time achieving the interpenetration
of architectural space and
environmental space (1960)'.
This design is an answer to the
Maison Particuliere by Van
Eesteren and Van Doesburg in
1923. The intention here was to
bring about a development towards
a more continuous spatiality in
three directions.

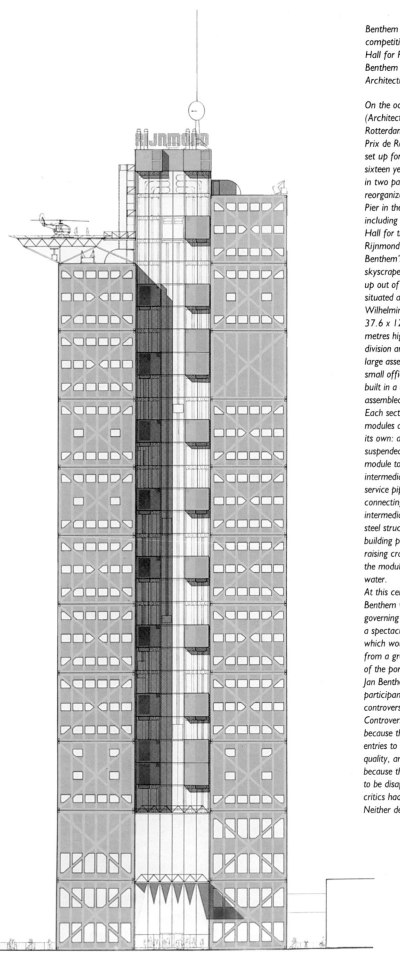

Benthem & Crouwel architects, competition design for a Provincial Hall for Rijnmond, design by J. Benthem for the Prix de Rome for Architecture, 1982.

On the occasion of the AIR (Architecture International Rotterdam) – festival in 1982, a Prix de Rome for Architecture was set up for the first time after sixteen years. The assignment was in two parts and consisted of the reorganization of the Wilhelmina Pier in the port of Rotterdam, including a design for a Provincial Hall for the future Province of Rijnmond.

Benthem's tower is a steel skyscraper, 120 metres high, built up out of prefabricated modules, situated at the head of the Wilhelmina Pier. The modules of 37.6 x 12.8 metres and 10.8 metres high allow flexible internal division and can be used both for large assembly rooms and for small offices. The modules can be built in a covered wharf and assembled on site.

Each section occupies a number of modules and has a central hall of its own: a 'sky-lobby', which is suspended between the two module towers and the intermediate zone, with lifts, service pipes and installations connecting the two towers. The intermediate zone, a prefabricated steel structure, is used during the building process as part of a self-raising crane which lifts and stacks the modules as they arrive by water.

At this central site in the port area, Benthem would have housed the governing authority of Rijnmond in a spectacularly constructed tower which would have been visible from a great distance. A metaphor of the port, a symbol of power. Jan Benthem was one of the two participants in the final run of a controversial Prix de Rome. Controversial, on the one hand because the jury considered the entries to be of insufficiently high quality, and on the other hand because the adjudication was felt to be disappointing and because critics had doubts about the brief. Neither design received the award.

In 'Building with Steel', nr. 62, March 1983, Rainer Bullhorst writes: 'To Benthem, honest expression is as important as proportion, at least in the constructive sense, although he never neglects the aesthetic factor. Only, his aesthetics are different from those of the Beaux Arts or the traditional Prix de Rome. His are the aesthetics of a functional, architectural and constructive synthesis. In that respect Benthem has made a statement with his non-award-winning Rijnmond building.'

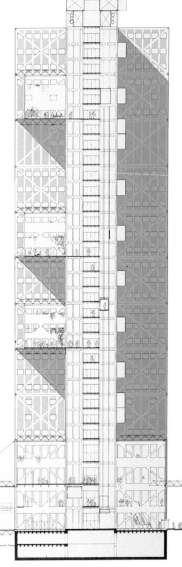

Acknowledgments to the following individuals and institutions for giving permission to publish drawings and photographs in their possession:

Municipal Archives, Amsterdam

Benthem, Crouwel architects, Amsterdam

P. Blom, Monnikendam

C. Boon, Amsterdam

Th. Bosch, Amsterdam

Architects Bureau Van den Broek & Bakema, Rotterdam

Bouw-es-wat-anders, Amsterdam

A. Cahen, Amsterdam

J. Coenen, Eindhoven

F.J. van Dongen, K. Oosterhuis, Delft

A. van Eyck, Loenen a/d Vecht

A. van Herk, S. de Kleyn, T. Kurvers & G. Urhahn, Amsterdam

H. Hertzberger, Amsterdam

H. Holzbauer, Amsterdam

J.P. Kloos, Haarlem

R. Koolhaas, London

Victor Nieuwenhuis, Amsterdam

Mevr. A. Oud-Dinaux, Wassenaar

Prentenkabinet (Print Room) Rijksmuseum, Leiden

H. Tupker, Amsterdam

C.J.M. van de Ven, Eindhoven

D. van Woerkom, Amsterdam

Other drawings from the collection of the Documentatiecentrum voor de Bouwkunst (Netherlands Documentation Centre for Architecture), Amsterdam.

Source material

Americana, cat. Rijksmuseum Kröller-Müller, Otterlo, 1975

Amsterdamse school, cat. Stedelijk Museum, Amsterdam, 1975

Architectura, cat. Stichting Architectuurmuseum, Amsterdam, 1975

Berlage, cat. Haags Gemeentemuseum, The Hague, 1975

H.P. Berlage, Uitbreidingsplan van 's Gravenhage (Development plan for The Hague), in: Bouwkunst, 1, 1909, p. 120

H.P. Berlage, Het Panthenon der Menschheid (The Pantheon of Mankind), pictures of the design, with text in verse by Henriëtte Roland Holst-Van der Schalk, Rotterdam, 1919

R. Brouwers, De volksvertegenwoordiging en het architectenvolk, Prijsvraaguitbreiding Tweede Kamer – een wedstrijd die voortijdig eindigde (Representation of the People and the Architectfolk, Competition for the extension of the Second Chamber – a competition that ended prematurely), The Hague, 1978

A. Cahen, Confrontation with a configuration, in: Open Research, The Hague, 1972

F.J. Duparc, Een eeuw strijd voor Nederlands cultureel erfgoed (A century of struggle for Netherlands cultural heritage), The Hague, 1975

Frederik van Eeden, Het Godshuis in de Lichtstad (The House of God in the City of Light), with draft designs by J. London, Amsterdam, 1921

Dr.Ir. J. Emmen, Ontwerp voor een oeververbinding over de Nieuwe Maas te Rotterdam (Design for a shore to shore link across the New Maas at Rotterdam), Amsterdam, 1936

Dr.Ir. J. Emmen, Tweede ontwerp voor een oeververbinding over de Nieuwe Maas te Rotterdam (Second design for a shore to shore link across the New Maas at Rotterdam), Amsterdam, 1936

Aldo van Eyck, projects 1962-1976, published by Johan van de Beek, Groningen, 1983

G. Fanelli, Modern architecture in the Netherlands 1900-1940, The Hague, 1978

Gedenkboek der Wagner Vereeniging (Memorial book of the Wagner Foundation), Amsterdam, 1934

A. van Herk and others, Stad aan het IJ, Oostelijk Havengebied (City on the IJ, Eastern Dock Area), Stichting Wonen, Amsterdam, 1980

Herman Hertzberger, Addi van Roijen-Wortmann, Francis Strauven, 'Aldo van Eyck', published by Stichting Wonen/Van Loghem Slaterus, Amsterdam, 1982

G. Hoogwoud, De Amsterdamse Beursprijsvraag (Competition for the Amsterdam Exchange) in: Nederlands Kunsthistorisch Jaarboek, 25, 1974, Bussum, 1975

W. Hutschenruyter, Het Beethovenhuis (The Beethoven House), Amsterdam, 1908

International competition of the Carnegie Foundation, Het Vredespaleis (The Palace of Peace), The Hague. The six prize-winning designs as well as forty other designs selected by the Maatschappij tot Bevordering der Bouwkunst (Society for the Promotion of Architecture), Amsterdam, 1906

Ir. E.J. Jelles & Ir. C.A. Alberts, Duiker, 1890-1935, in: Forum, 22, 1972, nr. 5 & 6

R. Koolhaas, Delirious New York, a retroactive manifesto for Manhattan, London, 1978

S. Moholy Nagy, Matrix of Man, An illustrated history of urban environment, London, 1968

New Babylon, cat. Haags Gemeentemuseum, 1974

F. Ottenhof, Goedkope Arbeiderswoningen (Cheap Labourers' dwellings), Rotterdam, 1936

J.J.P. Oud, Mein Weig in De Stijl, The Hague/Rotterdam, 1957-1958

A.W. Reinink, K.P.C. de Bazel architect, Leiden, 1965

H. Rosenau, The ideal city, in its architectural evolution, London, 1959

U. Conrads & H.G. Sperlich, Phantastische Architektur, Stuttgart, 1960

H. Rosenberg, De 19e eeuwse Kerkelijke Bouwkunst in Nederland (19th century church architecture in the Netherlands), The Hague, 1972

F.J. Sleeboom, Architektuurkritiek, een tragedie zonder einde (Architectural criticism, a tragedy without end), Plan, 1974, nr. 8, p. 9-30

City on Pampus, Forum, 1965, nr. 3

A. Sky & M. Stone, Unbuilt America, New York, 1976

I. Todd & M. Wheeler, Utopia, London, 1978

A.W. Weissman, Het Rijksmuseum te Amsterdam, Geschiedenis, In- en uitwendige versiering (The Rijksmuseum in Amsterdam, History, Interior and exterior decoration), Bouwstijl, Amsterdam, 1885

Other sources consulted are: architectural journals from the period 1850-1980 and the archives of the Nederlands Documentatiecentrum voor de Bouwkunst (Netherlands Documentation Centre for Architecture).